Some Borderland Gardens

Barbara Palmer
Alan Palmer

By the same authors

Some Shropshire Gardens

Some Borderland Gardens

Barbara & Alan Palmer

bridge
books
Wrexham

Published in Wales by
Bridge Books
61 Park Avenue
Wrexham, Clwyd
LL12 7AW

ISBN 1-872424-46-5

A CIP catalogue entry for this book
is available from the British Library

Front cover: Lady Cholmondely's Rose Garden, Cholmondeley Castle Gardens

Back cover: Monnington Court.

Printed and bound by
CPTS, Aberdeen
Hong Kong

Contents

N.B. The county names shown are those in use after local government reorganisation.

Foreword	7
Introduction	9
1. Abbey Dore Court — Herefordshire	11
2. Ashton Hayes — Cheshire	13
3. Branas Lodge — Denbighshire	14
4. Brilley Court — Herefordshire	16
5. Brobury House Gardens — Herefordshire	18
6. Bryn Derwen — Flintshire	19
7. Burford House Gardens — Worcestershire	21
8. Byeways — Shropshire	22
9. Cae Hywel — Powys	23
10. Chennels Gate — Herefordshire	25
11. Cherry Hill — Cheshire	26
12. Chirk Castle Gardens — Wrexham	29
13. Cholmondeley Castle Gardens — Cheshire	30
14. Craig Llyn — Powys	32
15. Cricklewood Cottage — Shropshire	34
16. Diamond Cottage — Powys	36
17. Dinben Isaf — Denbighshire	37
18. The Dingle — Powys	39
19. Dolwen — Powys	40
20. Erddig Park — Wrexham	42
21. Gardeners Lodge — Wrexham	43
22. Garth House — Powys	45
23. Glanwye — Powys	46
24. Gregynog — Powys	47
25. Hawarden Castle — Flintshire	49
26. Hergest Croft Gardens — Herefordshire	50
27. Hodnet Hall Gardens — Shropshire	52
28. Kyre Park Shrubbery — Worcestershire	54
29. Lightwood — Wrexham	55
30. Lingen Nursery and Garden — Shropshire	57
31. Llangedwyn Hall — Clwyd	58
32. Llysdinam — Powys	60
33. Maenllwyd Isaf — Powys	62

34. The Millers House — Powys 63
35. Monnington Court — Herefordshire 64
36. Ness Gardens — Cheshire 66
37. The Old Barn — Wrexham 67
38. Pen-y-Wern — Flintshire 69
39. Powis Castle Gardens — Powys 70
40. Radnor Cottage — Shropshire 73
41. River House — Wrexham 74
42. Strawberry Cottage — Herefordshire 75
43. Three Chimneys — Wrexham 77
44. Tir-y-Fron — Wrexham 78
45. Torwood — Herefordshire 80
46. Tyn-y-Graig — Denbighshire 81
47. The Walled Garden — Powys 83
48. The Weir Garden — Herefordshire 84
49. Welsh College of Horticulture — Flintshire 86
50. Woodside Cottages — Shropshire 87

Foreword

The border hills, Welsh mountains and rich red sandstone of Cheshire, Shropshire and Herefordshire are my home stomping ground. It is an exciting region in which to garden and to explore gardens. The growing season is generally cool and moist, helping to give flowers a longer display than in many southern and eastern counties and to keep foliage fresh deeper into the summer. The western fringes of the hills offer some very mild nooks, the valleys grow some of the country's finest oaks.

Many of the gardens in Barbara and Alan Palmer's book I know well. If you have not yet seen the yew battlements at Chirk, the jam-packed terraces at Powis Castle, the clematis at Burford House, the pastoral delights of Abbey Dore Court, or the hillside feats at The Dingle, you should, as the text indicates, warm up the jaloppy without delay. But there are many other gardens here that I don't know. The Palmers set the scenes appetisingly, observe sharply, and pass on plenty of snippets and tips. I shall enjoy sallying forth with their book in my pocket, and I am sure you will too.

Stephen Lacy

The gravel garden at Erway Farmhouse (the authors' garden).

Introduction

We are interested in Border gardens because we own one. The division between England and Wales – in our case the Shell Brook which soon finds its way to the River Dee – runs in a valley only a few hundred yards from the bottom of our paddock. How far the Borderlands extend is very much a matter of opinion and 'feel', but we have roughly defined it as the countryside about twenty miles either side of Offa's Dyke. This small area, the meeting place of every kind of landscape, from hill to valley, forest to plain, contains some of the most beautiful, diverse and unspoilt countryside left in the British Isles. There are still mountainous places in Scotland, Wales and Ireland where, even in midsummer, you can walk or drive miles without seeing another human being, but they become fewer every year, while lowland Britain is now scarred by new housing estates swamping tiny villages, out of town shopping developments or new roads. By definition therefore, Borderland gardens are country gardens, owned and loved by country people who treasure the history, topography and tranquillity of their unique and beautiful area. We must also confess a bias towards Mid and North Wales, the southern most garden covered being close to Ross-on-Wye. The northern most garden is Ness on the Wirral peninsula, where the border becomes the wide, muddy estuary of the Dee.

In spite of its turbulent history, or perhaps because of it, there are, surrounding some of the great Marcher castles, several large and important gardens which are described in this book. The bulk of the gardens however are small and intimate, one – or perhaps two – people's idealized landscape, escape hatch, or plant laboratory. Although many of the gardens are well known to us and therefore familiar in all seasons, some were visited only once and seen at only a single point in the gardening year. A description later or earlier would have produced a totally different angle with an alternative list of plants. We were also struck by the preponderance of good water gardens along the Border. These ranged from large lakes around which the whole garden revolved such as Hodnet and Monnington Court, to tiny, artificial, but no less interesting features like the one at Chennels Gate. One garden boasted a superb natural waterfall, while several had the great dividing rivers of the Border, the Dee, Severn and Wye (or their tributaries) close by.

Inevitably, we will have missed many good Border gardens through ignorance of their existence, the preference of their owners for complete privacy, or just lack of space. The Borderlands are rich in lovely gardens and this book could have been three times as long. Needless to say, the making of it was a real pleasure, not least because of the superb countryside in which the gardens lie. We hope it encourages others to leave their own plots for a day and venture into our beautiful Borderland.

Finally, thank you to everyone who allowed us into their gardens, often proffering coffee, lunch, even the odd gin and tonic (sadly we were usually in too much of a hurry to take advantage of the hospitality on offer), but especially to the National Trust, who care so well for some of the larger Border gardens. Most of all to those who gave so generously of their time, taking us on personal tours of their domain and narrating its history in ways so helpful to the writer and photographer.

Barbara and Alan Palmer

The Miller's House; an object lesson in how to change some decrepit buildings from eyesore to asset.

Abbey Dore Court Garden - Herefordshire

*A large and diverse garden bordered by the River Dore, containing a wealth of unusual plants.
Open daily from March to October (except Wednesday) as well as under the National Gardens
Scheme (see Yellow Book).*

Abbey Dore is a garden with everything. A gloriously peaceful setting in the Golden Valley
close to Hereford, an area renowned for its beautiful unspoilt countryside. An architecturally
distinguished house with interesting and picturesque outbuildings on a bank of the clear, clean,
River Dore. Superb trees, including a magnificent pair of *Sequoia gigantea* which must be
among the finest in the country. Two N.C.C.P.G. National Collections of sedum and euphorbia,
both displayed to advantage in wide beds and in company with other unusual herbaceous
perennials. A well sited pond backed by a rock garden on the far side of the river, reached by a
charming bridge. A wild garden; a dry, gravel garden; a fern border; sweeping lawns; and now,
a wonderful formal garden with a colour scheme suggested by that doyen of plantsmen, Graham
Thomas, it ranges from purple to gold, then through bluish-green, merging into silver at the far
end. This new garden is planted as much for foliage colour, shape, and texture, as bloom, and is
an absolute tour de force. It looks impressive after only a few years growth, before the larger
shrubs have really got going, and can only improve with age.

The new gold and silver garden at Abbey Dore designed by Graham Thomas.

Tall conifers shade hardy geraniums close to the river.

There are problems of course, even in a garden as well managed, maintained, and planted, as Abbey Dore. The river runs in a deepish channel, but floods in winter to leave layers of silt and carry away newly planted treasures. Also, gardeners know to their cost, that fertile soil which grows flowers to perfection also nurtures the strongest weeds. Since the family moved to Abbey Dore in 1967, finding little in the garden except the great trees and a mass of brambles, bindweed and ground elder, they have hacked and cleared, ploughed and planted, with very little outside help. Learning, by experience and making mistakes as they went along, how to get it right.

The old walled kitchen garden was tackled right at the start to provide fruit and vegetables for the house, while the first incursions into the ornamental garden did not begin until 1976. All this time the owners of Abbey Dore were also involved in dairy farming, which meant that little energy could be spared for gardening. Undaunted – as they were now getting many visitors, both individually and in groups – they began to convert the outbuildings into a tea room, gift gallery, shop and store room.

People come to Abbey Dore however to see the plants, and plants there are a plenty, right through the gardening year with a special emphasis on herbaceous perennials. It is hard to know where to begin, but in midsummer, my favourite season there, the peonies really steal the show. The owner states they were almost the very first things she planted and, after twenty-five years, they have built up into very impressive clumps. Peonies are best planted in very fertile soil and then left in peace, apart from a mulch of rotted manure now and then, as the specimens at Abbey Dore clearly indicate. Bowl of Beauty, with outer pink petals and a central boss of paler, narrower petals is outstanding, but the old fashioned, scented reds and pinks are hard to better, I also adore the white double, which has just a single petal of dark red in its pure centre, like a drop of blood.

There is a large collection of hardy geranium, which mostly flower with the peonies, also iris in many forms. I must say a word here in favour of *Iris* 'Gerald Darby', a subtle mauve, with elegant, sharply pointed buds, and grey-green foliage. The acid green of the euphorbia makes a backdrop for all the rich colours gathered in this part of the garden.

Scent is not neglected, chiefly from early buddleia such as *B.alternifolia*, and honeysuckle, but also the heavy, 'country' smell of elder, from *Sambucus nigra* 'Purpurea', a large shrub with the darkest purple foliage and the palest pink, flat plates of flower. Other plants noted in high summer range from the rarely seen galega, like a small, blue lupin (take care, it runs) to linaria. The latter needless to say, in its more uncommon pink form, Canon Went.

A wonderful garden indeed, the owners never putting a foot – or a plant – wrong, to create a truly memorable picture.

Ashton Hayes - Cheshire

A large valley garden including arboretum and ponds as well as rhododendrons and azaleas. Open under the National Gardens Scheme (see Yellow Book).

Following the three-quarter of a mile drive over low, undulating, rounded hills, populated by colonies of rabbits, to Ashton Hayes, one cannot help wondering exactly what one will find at the end of the path. The answer is a magical garden of enormous trees and mysterious pools, hidden in a deep cleft. Looking out from the manicured lawns to the front of the house, you have no idea of the delights awaiting in the lower valley garden.

At the top of the slope, close to the house, is a veritable giant of a tree, with broken, twisted limbs, pock-marked by woodpeckers or some huge beetle. Further down, are *Juniperus horizontalis*, Blue Spruce, and the smaller leaved rhododendrons. I liked the roses trained on rustic poles over the water; holding them away from the lake, while allowing them to be reflected in its water. Near this point, a low banked wall (I am sure an ancient ha-ha) shows the extent of the garden in the past.

Moving ever downwards to another lake on turf springy with moss, you pass massed ranks of tree heathers and great, pink-leaved pieris, untouched in their sheltered valley by night frosts. Here, in the lower bog garden, and contrasting vividly with the dwarf, blue rhododendrons (I am sure augustinii or Blue Tit) is the best stand of *Lysichiton americanus*, Yellow Skunk Cabbage, I have ever seen. This unusual plant appears early in the year, producing its large yellow, evil smelling spathes before the huge leaves. It likes a wet position, preferably in mud at the side of a pond, and the sight of the striking flowers far outweighs the awful smell: on the day we visited, the sun shone, making the vivid yellow carpet an unforgettable sight,

Much is made of the large leaved, variegated ivy, *Hedera canariensis*. It hides a strategically placed lake viewing

A magnificent stand of Lysichiton americanus, *the Yellow Skunk Cabbage, in a damp hollow at Ashton Hayes.*

13

seat, as well as climbing a double trunked tree to the extent that it was impossible to guess the variety of its host. A further bog is filled with a group of Giant Hogweed, *Heracleum mantegazzianum*, the browned skeletons like cart wheels on poles – I cannot believe they are any more impressive in full flower. One of the largest hardy perennials we can grow in this country, Giant Hogweed needs a damp place and lots of room. Take care, as the sap contains a poison which blisters the skin.

On the further, shady side of the valley, there is an underplanting of bamboo, so profuse, you almost expect a Giant Panda to emerge, the edges of the unusually wide leaf, has a pale brown marking, making an interesting contrast. It is similar to *Sasa veitchii*, an evergreen bamboo with purple stems. Here are choice small trees enjoying the moist shade; the shrimp pink, early growth of sycamore, as well as the delicate, hand-shaped new leaves of the Japanese acers.

The lakes are circled by a path which brings you back to the elevated house. There is a good deal of new tree planting underway, sheltered by a background of mature conifers. The young trees include cedar, columnar juniper, eucalyptus and Irish Yew, which will be magnificent when fully grown.

There is much to admire in this garden, from the deep indentations in the bark of an old oak, like nothing so much as Gothic carving, to the brash colour of the rhododendrons and azaleas.

Branas Lodge - Denbighshire

A medium sized hillside garden, with rhododendrons, azaleas, and a dramatic, natural waterfall. Open under the National Gardens Scheme (see Yellow Book).

Built in an elevated position overlooking the valley of the River Dee, nestling close up against the mountain, Branas Lodge has an enviable setting. It is made spectacular by a one hundred foot waterfall which falls sheer over the mountainside, then descends more slowly through the garden, ending in a landscaped pool just beside the house before continuing to the Dee. In the garden proper, every advantage is taken of this impressive natural topography.

At the time we visited, the rhododendrons and pieris were at their best, though this is by no means a one season garden. The conifers, deciduous trees, and a clipped holly hedge with projecting balls on stems for example, gives the front of the garden interest all year round. I was also impressed by the careful use of natural materials which blend so well with the wild hills all around. The confining walls are all local stone, similar to the house, and the terrace and steps made of Welsh slate. It is always worth taking the trouble to get this sort of detail right, as it adds so much to the final, overall garden picture. Even the stone barn boasted a beautifully crafted Welsh dragon weather vane.

Wild flowers are a feature close to where the garden begins to blend into the woods behind the house, primroses and bluebells on the hill, ferns close to the damp haze created by the waterfall, and a carpet of violets in the grass. I was struck by how good a plant gorse grown en masse is.

The waterfall at Branas Lodge has a drop of over 100 feet.

At Branas Lodge, a great clump makes a colourful patch of chrome yellow. If you are getting just one plant for a small garden, go for the double form, *Ulex europaeus* 'Flore Pleno', which bears masses of fragrant, pealike flowers in the spring.

There is no attempt at formality in this garden, and rightly so. Simple wooden bridges cross and recross the stream, leading to an adjoining hill dotted with more rhododendron and azalea. Sheltered beneath a huge pine, is another sitting out place with magnificent views of the surrounding mountains.

A natural stream, carefully channelled through the garden, becomes more formal as it nears the house.

The stone house looks so good in its hillside setting, it seems almost a shame to cover it, but true gardeners never have enough warm walls, and they are draped with many excellent climbers including *Clematis montana*, honeysuckle, and Virginia creeper, which give interest all year round. There is just a note of formality close to the terrace, where a stiff, rounded, grey-green willow grows close to the water. It could have been a weeping form, but somehow this garden manages to avoid all the cliches.

The raison d'etre of this garden is of course the waterfall; the garden is built around it, even the sound follows you wherever you walk. Who would dare attempt a 'Chelsea' style waterfall after seeing the natural beauty of Branas Lodge.

Brilley Court - Herefordshire

A medium sized walled garden with adjoining natural stream garden, in a beautiful setting close to the River Wye. Open under the National Gardens Scheme (see Yellow Book).

Brilley Court is not just a 'rose' garden, many other plants take the eye through the seasons, but in June it is a 'garden of roses'. The house is a large, traditional, stone and half-timbered building, but at the time we visited it was almost impossible to see, so covered are the walls with magnificent climbers. Most are roses, in apricot, pink and white, but also honeysuckle and *Jasminum officinale*.

Of all the gardens we visited, it seemed to me this garden would fulfil most people's ideal of a 'country' garden. The borders close to the house are filled with old cottage favourites such as nepeta, Catmint; campanula; *Crambe cordifolia*, like a white cloud against the blue sky; lupins;

hardy geraniums; purple sage: peonies; foxgloves, and of course, the roses. Mostly the shrub forms in soft pink, or that glorious mixture of red, mauve and grey that is so impossible to describe, the heavy, sweet perfume hanging in the air on a hot, still afternoon.

There is a flat terrace in the sheltered angle of two walls, and here a hint of sophistication appears, as the colour scheme is white. Roses; Madonna lilies and cistus in pots; pansies, white foxgloves, and the white *Fuchsia magellanica* 'Alba', which I find the hardiest of all. The 'country' atmosphere in this part of the garden, comes from the rampant, *Alchemilla mollis*, with its fluffy heads of green flowers and exquisitely shaped leaves, tying the whole scheme together, and avoiding an over-manicured look by seeding freely in all the cracks in the paving.

The terrace appears to be the only flat area in the garden, as the large lawn slopes down to a swimming pool, well camouflaged by walls and an old, converted outbuilding. There are groups of terracotta pots filled with lilies and a low fence draped with a montana clematis. Narrow paths at the bottom of the lawn disappear under banks of roses almost meeting in the middle, while the low stone walls again play host to further ramblers and climbers, until the scent and colour are almost over-powering.

Behind the swimming pool buildings is the vegetable garden and a most delightful cutting garden. The latter is always hard to manage well, as it is inevitably plundered of all its best blooms for the house. But at Brilley Court, even the utilitarian rows of Sweet William; sweet peas and delphiniums looked wonderful, while four honeysuckles, grown as standards, their trunks supported by strong posts, and appearing like small, scented, weeping trees were an absolutely perfect touch. Yet another good idea, on the cool side of the house, the roses were not yet out but the philadelphus were, cleverly prolonging the season and allowing a change of aroma from rose to orange blossom.

There is a wild garden, reached through a wrought iron gate overhung with *Rosa* 'Albertine', but even here, *Rosa rubrifolia* and foxgloves provide a link with the main garden. Mown paths point the way downwards to a marshy area with that impressive invader, Giant Hogweed in full

The white garden at Brilley Court.

flower. Some choicer trees are planted close to the main garden, l noted the tougher kinds of Japanese maple and some Tulip trees. Nearby, and leading from the top of the garden to the bottom, is a double row of fruit trees, beautiful in blossom and fruit, as well as providing a charming walk.

Technique in gardening is often confused with talent. People can always learn how to grow plants well, but whether they can create a real 'garden' is another matter. At Brilley Court beautifully arranged, flourishing plants come together to make a breathtaking whole.

Brobury House - Herefordshire

A large, park-like garden on a beautiful site, containing many magnificent trees. Open all year, Monday to Saturday. Phone:(01981) 500229.

Although Brobury House garden contains very few bedding plants, its meticulous maintenance and somewhat complicated layout gives it the air of a Victorian garden. This impression is emphasized by the house, built in 1880 of grey stone and sporting turrets, french doors, a conservatory and a Gothic portico in true Victorian style. It was no surprise to learn that both house and garden were the setting for the television drama *Dandelion Dead*, set in the period just after the First World War.

Neptune with his trident guards the long pond at Brobury House.

When the property was purchased by the present owners in the early 1970s, they did find a Victorian garden of annuals, as well as an over abundance of rose trees – three thousand to be precise – but these were swiftly removed. The object was to create a much more natural ambience, in keeping with the beautiful country all around and the many superb trees already on the site. The statuary, graceful flights of steps, and most important of all, the large, grey house dominating the top of the slope, will always retain a Victorian or Edwardian flavour in the garden however, no matter how it is altered.

The wide, flat lawn at the side of the house is the site for three huge cedars – *Cedrus atlantica* 'Glauca', the Blue Atlas cedar: *C.libani,* the Cedar of Lebanon: and *C.deodara.* These trees, as well as all the others at Brobury, are now at the height of their beauty, having grown to maturity in what must be almost perfect conditions, and receiving regular attention of pruning and maintenance since the day they were planted. They were also laid out originally by someone with an expert's eye for how they would appear a hundred years hence, as they are placed to perfection. I might add that the present owners continue to stock the garden with beautiful trees and shrubs. A particularly charming sunken area contains four weeping beech, *Fagus sylvatica purpurea* 'Riversii', sheltered by a grove of *Betula Papyrifera*, the Paper birch, with startling white trunks. Another tree which cannot fail to be noticed, is a truly stupendous oak, which pre-dates the house by two hundred years and stands on the periphery of the garden. The girth is enormous, while the canopy must cover a huge area. From a seat

Two unusual weeping copper beech trees, with Brobury House in the background.

beneath the branches there are beautiful views across the Wye to a vicarage that was for a short time the home of the Rev. Francis Kilvert, the noted diarist.

There are several formal ponds in the garden, as well as a natural boggy area with ligularia and bulrushes. I very much admired the long canal, with Neptune in weathered grey stone, complete with trident, guarding one end. So often this kind of formal statuary can look pretentious, unless perfectly executed and placed. At Brobury, the figure is at one with its setting, and provides just the right finishing touch.

Also in this area is one of the largest parrotia I have ever seen. *Parrotia persica*, is usually sold and planted as a large shrub for autumn colour, the huge example at Brobury must be quite a sight when the leaves turn. Its plain leaves are set off by a nearby Sweet gum, *Liquidambar styraciflua*, with maple-shaped leaves, also noted for its autumn dress, when the leaves turn brilliant shades of orange, red, and purple. To complete the picture, the owners have added a pair of *Robinia pseudoacacia* 'Frisia', in buttercup-yellow.

You can actually explore the garden and its surroundings from the comfort of Brobury House, as it is now run as a country house hotel.

Bryn Derwen - Flintshire

A half acre old walled garden wth large sunken area, full of interesting plants. Open under the National Gardens Scheme (see Yellow Book).

Bryn Derwen is a pleasant family house close to Mold, with a small, well planted front garden. Conventional enough you might think, but a surprise awaits you when you walk around the house to look at the rear garden. The whole area at the back of the house falls away from your feet, and you look down on what can only be described as an amphitheatre, the 'seats' on which the Romans might have sat, now planted up with a wonderful collection of hardy perennials.

Surrounding houses and high walls give the whole garden a sheltered air, but it is far from easy to cultivate, being very hot in the summer, and a frost pocket in the winter. Opinions differ about the origin of the depression. It feels like an old quarry, except that the floor is flat and it is hardly deep enough. Perhaps it was only used for local purposes, or to build Bryn Derwen itself? Though the owner believes that it may have been a stock yard for sheep when the outskirts of Mold were a good deal more rural than they are today. Whatever its origins, the owner has made the most of the advantages and skilfully seeks to overcome the difficulties.

The large central lawn is broken by a terraced area, sheltered by climber hung trellis to give shade and provide a framework for scented plants. There is a seat from which to admire the garden, and a small pond swarming with tadpoles. I very much admired the beautiful stand of *Iris sibrica*, one of the easiest and most reliable of all the tall iris in a damp border. Also doing well, was the mauvey-blue Potato vine, *Solanum jasminoides*. There is a white form, *S.jasminoides* 'Album', but it is decidedly tender, and I don't think flowers quite as profusely.

There are in fact several small ponds in the garden, another in an area given over to Japanese plants. Not a Japanese garden strickly speaking, but acers, hosta, and other plants from Japan,

A secluded corner, perfect for sitting out at Bryn Derwen.

growing together informally. I liked the gravel garden for sprawlers, an idea I use myself, but the owner of Bryn Derwen has gone further, putting a sheet of plastic under the gravel to suppress weed growth, which I thought an excellent notion.

Planting is crowded, but well thought out and placed. The sloping beds around the garden help in showing the flowers and foliage to advantage, the walls at the top making for a good background. The walls are not wasted of course. I noted many tender climbers including a superb ceanothus. When visiting gardens, I have often met with the glorious, dark-blue, *Ceanothus impressus* 'Italian Skies', so it was interesting to make the acquaintance of Cascade, equally impressive, but just a shade or two lighter. A very unusual buddleia, also grown against the wall for maximum protection, is the somewhat tender, *Buddleia colvilei* 'Kewensis'. It has large, raspberry coloured flowers, and is indeed the largest flowered buddleia capable of surviving out-of-doors in Great Britain. This species also makes a wonderful show, each branch laden with small, dark-red, pointed flowers.

There is even room in the garden for a wilder area, where bulbs, ferns and a Rowan flourish. Also a whole bed set aside for some of the rarer hosta, including: Frances Williams, with yellow-edged leaves; Halcyon, a particular favourite, with neat, heart-shaped, blue-grey leaves; Blue Angel and Blue Wedgewood, among the best of the 'blue' hosta. Shaded in just the way hosta enjoy by the branches of an old pear tree, and carefully edged by the dead wood from another, this bed summed up the thought and attention to detail which has gone into the making of the whole garden.

Burford House Gardens - Worcestershire

A large and influential 1950s garden, renowned for its displays of herbaceous perennials and clematis. Garden open daily in the spring and summer, nursery open all year, but restricted opening during the winter months. Phone (01584) 810777.

Although created only forty years ago by the three Treasure brothers, Burford House Garden has an important place in gardening history. It was one of the first gardens to experiment with the notion of island beds for herbaceous plants and shrubs, instead of the familiar long border usually backed by wall or hedge (this idea was also developed by the Bloom family in The Dell Garden at Bressingham). Exponents of this technique, claim that plants grow stronger and sturdier without backing, which tends to 'draw' the plants, making them taller and more susceptible to wind. The shorter, bushier plants in open ground therefore need less staking.

Conventional borders also feature at Burford however, as do the Stream Garden, the Courtyard Garden, the Summer Garden, and many more. All these separate gardens developed over a long period, as the garden gradually expanded to over four acres of year round delight.

The original idea was to create a garden where young plants on sale in the adjoining nursery could be viewed when mature. Also to show visitors the many ways clematis could be exploited in a garden setting growing through shrubs, as ground cover, or mixed with herbaceous plants in the border for example – Treasures having become a specialist clematis nursery and holder of the National Collection. John Treasure, the brother most responsible for the way the gardens appear today, succeeded famously in spite of many early problems, which included hard winters ('62 and '83), flooding from the nearby River Teme which borders one third of the garden, and some early mistakes in the placing of trees; which turned out too tall, poorly shaped, or too close. Which gardener in the world has not made the last error?

I have known the garden over a long period, and never fail to garner inspiration from a visit, as well as finding some new plant to covert for my own garden (the last visit introduced me to *Houttuynia cordata* 'Flore Pleno', a double white form of this delightful ground spreader for a damp place). The whole garden in fact, excels in inspired plant combinations, with the most imaginative use of colour. Although the soil tends to the limey side of neutral, some acid lovers such as kalmia will flourish, as the top layers are magnesium rich. Also, the soil, replenished by the flooding river and an ample supply of moisture, makes the garden very fertile.

A late visit to Burford, when most gardens were looking tired and wilted after a boiling summer, produced as many fresh ideas as early spring. Late, warm colour from groups of inula, spiraea, and sidalcea. *Hydrangea sargentiana*, astilbe, and hosta enjoying the moisture and

The gardens at Burford were created in the 1950s around this superb Georgian house.

Hosta, Alchemilla mollis, *polygonum, and lysimachia make a stunning composition of flowers and foliage.*

cool shade close to the river. Wands of pink and white dierama, Angel's fishing rod, waving in the breeze, perfectly set off against a dark plum rhus. A wall full of yellow corydalis, and, growing over the wall, the rare and desirable Clematis 'Sir Trevor Lawrence'. Imagine a group of purple and red lily tulips backed by lush foliage, gracefully draped, to visualise this wonderful plant.

The Courtyard Garden is on two levels, with an oblong pond, and self-seeding erigeron carpeting the connecting steps. There are rare and tender treasures protected by the walls and the house. Itea, with its long, trailing catkins: the Bottlebrush, *Callistemon rigidus*, and Arum lilies in the water. Also in this area, two further clematis for which genus Burford is justly famous, *Clematis florida* 'Sieboldii', with passion-flower-like, white blooms and a purple centre, and its even rarer sister, *C.florida* 'Alba Plena', a subtle greeny-white.

Byeways - Shropshire

A medium sized, plantswomans garden, containing a superb collection of rare and unusual plants. Open under the National Gardens Scheme in combination with other Whittington gardens (see Yellow Book).

The garden at Byeways is a storehouse of plants for a hobby that began as an interest and ended as a business. The owner has a degree in horticulture, but began twenty-five years ago as a flower arranger with a particular interest in dried flowers. She lectured at clubs and W.I. meetings, and was often asked about the unusual plants she incorporated in her creations. This led in time to propagating and selling the plants, until the market stall where the products of the Byeways garden end up, has become *the* place to find that difficult to get, or rare flower.

There are some mature trees at Byeways, but the main garden is mostly filled with a wonderful collection of herbaceous perennials in large island beds and a grit mulched area. The beds are carefully placed to give a variety of growing conditions, as the plants come first, their likes and dislikes all carefully considered.

Although the soil is mainly light and well-drained, the large scree bed is ideal for plants which dislike any damp around the collar. Standing out when we visited in late June was the pink poppy, *Papaver orientale* 'Turkish Delight', a truly luscious colour, the petals like finest tissue paper. *Fibigia clypeata* is small and unobtrusive-until you look closely. It resembles nothing so much as a cactus with flat seed pods on each side of a long stem. The owner of Byeways says the earlier yellow flowers are full of interest too. *Gillenia trifoliata* was a revelation, with delicate white flowers set off by dark orange stems. This is another plant which prolongs its season by looking as good after flowering as before.

The plants at Byeways have been collected over many years, some just by chance, gifts from friends, or being in the right place at the right time. A truly remarkable variegated rose for example, was picked up from an ordinary market stall. I am familiar with the variegated *Rosa wichuraiana* 'Variegata', which has cream, pink and green leaves and a small, pink flower, but the specimen at Byeways is a typical H. T. rose with a dark pink flower. It is extraordinary to think that it is not in commerce.

In a cool, damp bed, grow the Blackthorn strain of *Helleborus x.sternii*. This form has a delightful leaf, with a definite and very attractive blue-grey tinge. A favourite plant in my own garden is *Dactylorrhiza elata*, the purple orchid. It never fails to create a sensation when visitors see our large clumps in all their glory. At Byeways I saw a better form, *Orchis mascula* 'Early Purple', with even larger flowers and a spotted leaf.

If I have given the impression that this garden is just a collection of flowers, nothing could be further from the truth. The garden blends well with the modern house; there is an oval pond, a bubble fountain, a terrace with carpeting plants and self-seeding alpines. Scent comes from a *Cytisus battandieri*, flowering its heart out against

The pond is surrounded by alpine plants in scale with its small size.

the wall. But ones eye is constantly drawn back to the herbaceous beds. The lilies, sheltered by a tall hedge; the dwarf grasses in beautifully compact clumps; a vast collection of penstemons and hardy geraniums. The lovely leaf shapes of artemisia, and a magnificent *Salvia argentea* dominating it's area. The latter incidentally, grown from seed. One can only admire the industry and knowledge which makes this garden and its contents so fascinating a place for the true plantsman or woman.

Cae Hywel - Powys

A small garden on different levels, with herb and rock areas. Open under the National Gardens Scheme (see Yellow Book).

I struggle to grow primroses, the owner of Cae Hywel has them coming up between the stones in her drive! And not only there our native yellow primrose, *Primula vulgaris*, has seeded itself in grass, along the edges of borders, and especially in the large herb and kitchen garden to the rear of the house. This self-seeding is in keeping with the ethos of the whole garden, which

An almost life-size figure of Pan decorates the garden at Cae Hywel.

makes no attempt to be anything other than a simple, country plot.

The red brick Victorian house is in a slightly elevated position at the edge of a small village, though it has the neat air of a town dwelling. The veranda at the front plays host to a magnificent wisteria, the twisting stems as intricate as the wrought iron which supports it. There is a terrace with steps down to a small lawn, but here all formality ends, the sides and rear of the house mostly being laid down to lawn with fruit trees grown as much for blossom as the autumn fruit. *Fritillaria meleagris*, the Snake's-head fritillary and daffodils, are naturalised in the grass underneath them. Although they look delicate, with their chequered bells in mauve and white hanging on slender stems, Snake's-head fritillary are in fact excellent subjects for naturalising, provided the soil is not too dry.

Close to a small pond stands the most superb lead figure of Pan, looking completely at home amidst trees and water, sporting budding horns, pipes and tiny tail. His accompanying nymph hides coyly around the corner, the artist who sculpted them asking that they should always be sited slightly out of sight as if searching for one another.

There is some little formality at the back of the house in the shape of a square kitchen and herb garden (the owner of Cae Hywel once sold herbs at local fairs and is well versed in all their lore). It is sheltered by a brick wall and thick hedges, making it a wind free sun trap. Peaches are trained on the wall, and I was interested to learn that their grower is never troubled by peach leaf curl. She firmly believes that this is because of the garlic, Welsh onion and chives, she has planted around them. The pungent smell – increased by trampling whenever she passes by – seems to inhibit the pest.

Many varieties of herb are grown in long, oblong beds, with grass paths between, some edged with clipped lavender. I particularly admired the large stands of comfrey, and the combination of young, bright green chives, with the pinky-brown growth of bronze fennel; just as good to eat as the green sort, and twice as pretty.

Other notable plants include a *Davidia involucrata*, the Handkerchief tree, with large, white bracts on mature specimens in spring. It was planted as a sizeable tree, but the owner of Cae Hywel still had to wait fifteen years for the first flowering. I must also mention that other great self seeder, *Meconopsis cambrica*, the Welsh poppy, in both orange and lemon shades, which takes over when the primroses fade. Not to every ones taste I know, as it can be something of a weed if it really likes the conditions, but a first class wild garden plant. Get the double form if you prefer a tidy garden or are restricted for space. Again, just as good, and with only a quarter of the seed to contend with.

Chennels Gate Garden - Herefordshire

A two acre, plantsman's, cottage garden, with small nursery ajoining. Open throughout the year, and for the National Gardens Scheme (see Yellow Book). Phone: (01544) 327288.

Chennels Gate is a new garden, created in the past four years. Friendly and intimate, it surrounds a cream and black painted Victorian house which it compliments to perfection. The entire garden is set within fifteen acres of pasture, which the owners have laid down to orchard and woodland, while the area around the house is divided into separate, small gardens, each with its own particular theme.

The large lawn in the front of the house has mature, box-edged borders, and it was interesting to see a new, round rose bed, encircled with tiny young box plants. Two ideas I particularly admired in this part of the garden were a very large tree stump (almost all of the tree up to where the branches had sprouted), covered by two rampant climbers – *Clematis montana*, and the Golden Hop. The yellow foliage of the latter contrasted beautifully with the dark leaves of the montana, which I guessed from the colour was rubens. *And* you still have the flowers to admire in May. I must warn that you will need a very big stump for this combination however.

The second good idea is close to the conservatory at the side of the house. Here, just outside the door to be exact, is a most attractive water feature. An old pump has been plumbed to provide a constant flow of water, broken by slates and rocks as well as a stone bowl with a hole. The flow ends in a small, brick, raised pond, with space to sit and dangle your fingers in the water. There are rare ferns enjoying the moisture, as well as numerous pigeons and doves popping in for a drink as we admired quite the most delightful bird bath I have ever seen

The garden is flat, though there are views of hills all around, and the owners have wisely paid particular attention to the divisions in the garden trellis, hedge, and espalier fruit trees, successfully hiding one part from another. An informal mix of herb, cottage garden and orchard, lies to one side of the house. It is planned as a series of long beds with very little grass. A completely prostrate, fallen apple tree, still flourishing and producing fruit, has its trunk planted with ivy and ferns. Although lying on its side, the roots are firm in the ground, making it an extraordinarily effective focal point. *Achillea filipendulina* 'Gold Plate', and *Cynara cardunculus*, Cardoon, in full flower, make a striking combination of purple and gold close by, with an underplanting of hosta at their feet.

It was wonderful to see this part of the garden alive with butterflies and

A delightful pool at Chennels Gate is a magnet for all the surrounding wildlife on a hot summer's day.

hover wasps. The latter were attracted to all the flowering herbs, origanum, lavenders, mints and fennel.

There is more formality on the other side of the house, though the soft cheep of hairy legged chickens and their brood always reminds you that this is very much a country garden. I thought the small rose garden, though completely green when we visited in late August, a lesson in restraint and good planting. The focal point in this secret garden is an old chimney pot, the sides of the plot defined by posts with rope swags. Shrub rose hedges enclose this area, giving it a completely different, cut off feeling from the rest of the garden.

Close to the house, an exotic touch comes from an orange tree in a pot, covered in fruit, as well as a gravel garden with random gravel paths and small, neat beds, given over to the more tender perennials. In fact, most tender plants are grouped close to the house with piptanthus, *Convolvulus mauritanicus*, penstemons, and *Verbena bonariensis* enjoying the protection, and adding to the beauty of this interesting garden.

Cherry Hill - Cheshire

A large country garden comprising woods, lake, rhododendrons, herbaceous borders, ornamental vegetable garden and views. Open under the National Gardens Scheme (see Yellow Book).

Cherry Hill is a large country garden containing many different areas, the whole knitted together by a network of walls, hedges and gravel paths. The silvery-grey, timber framed house dominates the main garden, which slopes down to a rhododendron and azalea filled hollow containing a large natural pond. It is divided by a bridge which is really a dam, separating the wilder, distant bank with gunnera and Dogwood from the more colourful garden.

The soil must be very acid, as the rhododendron and azaleas, interestingly inter-mingled on one bank with halesia, were thriving. The shelter provided by the lie of the land, mature trees, ample moisture from the pond and a natural spring, must also help to account for the healthy green leaves and superb flowers on all the plants in this area. From the house on the top of the

Spectacular use of the hardy Geranium *'Johnson Blue' at Cherry Hill.*

26

slope, the eye drops down across massed banks of brilliant colour from the rhododendrons (once cut off by a ha-ha) then past meadows and burgeoning hedges to a distant view of the Welsh hills.

This part of the garden alone, is enough to make Cherry Hill memorable, but a gap in a yew hedge at the side of the house, leads one into a wholly different picture. Here, the slope is gentle, the mood formal and enclosed, providing a perfect

The 'wild' rhododendron and pool garden makes a welcome contrast to the formal garden.

contrast. It is a garden of hedges, mainly beech, box and yew, with the added advantage of a high, sheltering wall running along one complete side of the garden, past the house and ending in a group of farm buildings built of the same weathered brick. Hedges run parallel and at an angle, enclosing separate gardens, while the box, clipped neat and low, contains a magnificent bed of roses and the ornamental vegetable garden. Here, practicality is not lost to ornament however, all the vegetables are both visually appetizing and edible, though they are mixed with flowering chives, colourful sages, wigwams of sweet peas, and great stands of angelica. The curving brick paths might seem merely decorative, but also enable the owners to pick vegetables and herbs dry shod.

Planting is simple and effective throughout this part of the garden. The owner is not afraid to use large quantities of one plant. *Geranium* 'Johnson's Blue' for example, quite one of the best of the hardy geranium, is used down the entire length and both sides of one, long, enclosed path. Blue delphiniums backed by copper beech hedges and peonies in season, complete an unforgettable picture. The border continues the other side of a bisecting path with just the red peonies; perfectly simple, but so right.

Another, difficult, triangular area, had once again been contained with box, given a viewing seat beneath a clematis bower, crossed by a gravel and stone path, then filled with chamomile. It looked so fresh and green, even out of flower, and is the ideal, calming contrast to the showy clematis. Moving on to an oblong lawn, this time surrounded by a wall and beech hedge, a central round is planted with Silver-leaf pear, *Pyrus salicifolia* 'Pendula', encircled by lavender. Fruit trees cling to the walls in this part of the garden, but the predominant planting is of climbing roses, mostly the old fashioned, heavy headed forms, in pinks, mauves and reds.

Every corner brings fresh delights, the whole garden exhibiting a natural, unlaboured air, yet meticulously cared for. I would not have changed a single plant throughout, nor could I have altered a hedge or a path for the better.

The Hawk House, burnt to the ground in 1977, but now fully restored.

Chirk Castle Gardens - Wrexham

Four and a half acres of trees, lawns, and flowering shrubs, contained by magnificent yew topiary, all surrounding one of the finest castles in the Borderland. Owned by The National Trust, and open frequently in season. Also for the National Gardens Scheme (see Yellow Book).

Chirk Castle is a remarkably well preserved, monumental, late thirteenth century Marcher castle, which has had a number of garden layouts throughout its turbulent history. The trees in the park have also been replanted and felled many times, while the whole area was totally redesigned by William Emes in 1764 (who also had a hand in Powis and Erddig Park, as well as other, less well known gardens in Wales.)

The owners of Chirk tended to follow the prevailing garden fashions over the years. Sir Thomas Myddleton in 1653 for example, made a formal layout of gravel walks, lawns and neatly enclosed areas bordered with clipped yew. In the mid eighteenth-century, when the Capability Brown enthusiasm was at its height, a landscaped pleasure park with ha-ha and carefully placed groups of trees was created. The great yew hedges which so perfectly mimic the massive outline of the castle, with battlements and simple rounded shapes like ancient megaliths, were planted in 1872. Their strange, sugar loaf shapes and dense green colour, contrasts with the vivid green of the grass and grey stone castle. I felt that you could walk easily on their flattened tops and slide down their sloping sides.

There is a bright spring border close to the castle wall, with annual honesty; wallflowers *Bellis perennis* 'Dresden China' and tulips, as well as roses to come. But the overall impression in this part of the garden, is of formal, green magnificence, perfectly in keeping with the backdrop of the castle. Steps down to a sloping lawn guarded by two bronze nymphs, lead to a very different garden picture.

Early in the year, snowstorms of pale-pink blossom from *Prunus* 'Kanzan' float in the breeze. It is an old suburban favourite some think a little garish, but at Chirk, its pink flowers and dark foliage is toned down by the woody background. High yew hedges, well clipped, but this time fleshy and rounded, made an impressive feature, concentrating the colour of *Acer pseudoplatanus* 'Brilliantissimum' in front, always tricky to place with its vibrant, shrimp-pink, early foliage. I also loved the contrast between the enormous billowing, cerise rhododendrons, and the sharp formality of a Cedar of Lebanon. Other fine trees in this area include one of the earliest plantings of *Larix decidua*, Common Larch; *Magnolia salicifolia*; and a quite wonderful Himalayan Whitebeam, *Sorbus aria* 'Michellii'. We were lucky enough to see the latter in very early leaf, when it is surely at its most beautiful.

A summer house, which has a conspicuous position on the Lower Lawn, has also seen many reincarnations, having variously been a conservatory, a mews for falcons (hence Hawk House, its present title) and a 'Green House'. It was totally rebuilt after a fire in 1977.

The Shrub Garden to the front of the Hawk House is sited in a slight depression and sheltered by belts of mature trees, thereby allowing many exotics to be grown not normally possible in North Wales. I was amazed to see a fair sized *Crinodendron hookerianum*, covered in promising

Chirk Castle, with meticulously clipped yews standing guard.

buds. This beautiful small tree has the darkest possible evergreen leaves and scarlet hanging lanterns in the spring. As it produces its buds in the autumn, and holds them ready to expand in April or May, the slightest frost disrupts its pattern of flowering. This crinodendron is carefully placed in an excellent position, nestling close to a holly with other sheltering trees around.

Here, the garden is arranged in glades, with many large island beds of azalea, rhododendron and pieris, underplanted with hosta, astlbe and primroses. For me, its greatest glory is a Handkerchief tree in full bloom. There is a group of *Magnolia x.soulangeana* in white and pinky-mauve; a pool with Japanese acers dipping their leafy fingers into the water; one constantly meets treasures around every corner.

Behind the Hawk House is a large rockery with that other coverted exotic so difficult to grow away from the milder coast, *Embothrium coccineum*, the Chilean Firebush. Even Bodnant Garden lost its large specimens in the hard winter of 1982, how did the ones at Chirk survive?

This part of the garden, after the carefully tended rockery, blends into a more informal wooded, rhododendron plantation. One group of bushes in particular, colour blended in shades of pink and peach, backed by the new foliage of a copper beech, will remain long in my memory. The whole garden in fact remains as a distinct series of pictures, from the studied formality close to the castle, to the wilder areas and the great trees; though on the spot, all blends imperceptibly into one, wonderful whole.

Cholmondeley Castle Gardens - Cheshire

A magnificent landscaped park, including fine trees and an extensive water garden. Open regularly throughout the season, also under the National Gardens Scheme (see Yellow Book). Tel: (01829) 720383.

The gardens at Cholmondeley Castle are extensive, thelr periphery, with the aid of drives, woods and ha-ha, blending imperceptibly into the beautiful Cheshire countryside all around. Every part of the garden is memorable, from the great, pinky-grey stone castle superbly sited on the brow of a gentle hill, to the picturesque Temple Garden, where water, beautiful buildings, islands, water-lilies, bridges, trees and rocks, come together in a magical landscape composition,

The picture I still carry in my minds eye however, is of the mature trees in the park: native species-oak, lime and yew, as well as the exotic – Monkey Puzzle, Japanese maples, and great, flat tiers of cedar of Lebanon. This superb treescape, with almost as much colour and shape as a flower bed, contrasts leaping yellow flames of Irish Yew, with the drooping green branches of enormous weeping deciduous trees. The blues of junipers, against deep green shadows lit up by the sunlight on individual pale leaves. Some of the larger trees, the cedar of Lebanon, swamp cypress and wellingtonia, are thought to be contemporary with the castle, built by the 1st Marquess of Cholmondeley between 1801 and 1804.

In the glade below the castle, huge island beds of bamboo make a graceful background for many herbaceous perennials. There is much use of lilies in the lightly shaded areas beneath trees; martagon types seem especially successful. I do not wish to make this description sound like a plant catalogue, but mention must be made of quite the largest Mount Etna broom, *Genista aetensis*, I have ever seen, also a beautiful single white rose, 'Wickwar', with golden stamens, pale green foliage and an exquisite scent, close to the terrace wall.

The aforementioned terrace, is a sheltered spot with many tender, sun loving plants clustering against the walls. Agapanthus, the seeds of which came to Cholmondeley straight from South Africa: hebes in variety; ceanothus; phlomis and *Senecio greyi*. Red and pink valerian, actually growing in the wall, gives a delightful touch of informality.

A garden of this size and complexity brings many problems, not the least of which are recurrent plagues of rabbits. These were a special trial when the rose garden with its attendant herbaceous beds were first laid out in the 1950s. The whole area having to be fenced until established. It is now however, filled with scent and colour from many types of roses, all chosen, by trial and error, to suit the light, drought prone, typical Cheshire sand. The centre piece is a sundial, surrounded by lavender, and set off by four double arches supporting ramblers. There are standard roses, formal beds — again edged with lavender — and huge climbers clinging to the tennis court net alongside. Two magnolias give colour and scent before the roses bloom. The double herbaceous borders also contain roses, linking them with the formal paved garden, though when we visited in July, great spikes of delphinium; *Campanula lactiflora*; salvia; echinops and nepeta, were producing a symphony of blues and making it hard to believe by their flourishing condition that the soil is so very poor in this area, I thought the four weeping silver pears, *Pyrus salicifolia* 'Pendula', neatly clipped, an inspired finishing touch, setting off the ends of the borders perfectly.

One comes upon the Temple Garden, by passing through a stone gatehouse and looking down towards a water-lily filled lake, containing two grassy islands connected to the mainland by simple wooden bridges the larger island dominated by a stone building. It came originally from the gardens of the Old Hall, and is echoed by another, circular temple, with a wrought iron roof. This is placed near the edge of the garden where the dark green background shows

The Temple Garden at Cholmondeley Castle.

The double herbaceous borders leading to the Rose Garden in midsummer glory.

off the pale stone pillars to perfection, while the intricate iron roof is seen against the brightness of the sky. Simply furnished in green, with just trees, grass and architecture, this garden would be outstanding, but it is also thoughtfully planted to enhance every changing season.

Early in the year, spring bulbs such as crocus and daffodils decorate the scene, to be followed by azaleas and dwarf rhododendron. Later, the giant gunnera makes its presence felt, and the summer shrubs such as philadelphus, *Rosa* 'Nevada', and buddleia add scent as well as colour. Needless to say, the autumn tints are spectacular.

A walk around the lake produces many delightful vignettes; a small waterfall with hosta and a well placed stone heron swallowing fish; *Acer griseum*, showing off its wonderful, tan coloured, peeling bark; Koi carp of enormous size and flashing metallic scales rippling the water as they push the water-lilies aside. And always the rare and wonderful trees *Arbutus x.andrachnoides*; *Catalpa bignonioides; Parrotia persica,* best of all for autumn colour; many magnolias, and a fine *Metasequoia glyptostroboides*, a deciduous conifer only discovered in China in the 1940s. This is to mention but a few.

In a garden so full of striking vistas and unusual plants, much must inevitably be left out. I have not even touched on the Cherry Walk; the Silver Wedding Arboretum, with more interesting trees; Tower Hill, or the great, white gates at the end of the main drive. I can only advise, not just to pay one visit, but to repeat the pleasure throughout the gardening season, I can guarantee that you will never be disappointed.

Craig Llyn - Powys

Two acres of steep, hillside garden overlooking the River Wye, with an outstanding collection of early shrubs. Open under the National Gardens Scheme (see Yellow Book).

A garden needs love as well as landscaping, time and thought as well as money spent on it. Craig Llyn has had all of these things and more beside. The first owner was faced with a rocky hillside on which he built a wooden, two-storey house to use as a holiday home, mainly to go fishing in the River Wye, which runs close by in the valley. Stories are told about his gardening partner leaning out of a window upstairs to get a bird's-eye-view, and directing the placing of the stones found on the site with awful precision and a tendency to Zen Buddhist theories. The result is a wonderfully natural garden, anchored to the hillside by many rocky paths, some made beautiful by moss growing over and between the cracks. Wild flowers also seed in and around the whole garden, especially bluebells, foxgloves, ferns and the smaller flowered hardy geraniums.

The original builder was a retired tea planter, and I can only believe that the rocky hills and profusion of dark leaved rhododendron with which he filled the garden, reminded him of India. The present owner continues the good work. She has lived there for eighteen years, and her first task was to rescue the garden from an overgrowth of brambles and ferns. The bones, in the shape of the many paths and sculptural rocks, were all there waiting to be discovered however, and she has made the most of her bounty.

As well as a notable collection of rhododendron and azalea, there are many other interesting plants in the garden. For me, the *piece de resistance*, is an enormous Chinese witch hazel, *Hamamelis mollis*. Having grown this outstanding, scented, winter-flowering shrub myself, I know it develops at a snails pace. The specimen at Craig Llyn is all of twenty feet high, and as much through. The owner is able to pick great bunches to scent the house at Christmas without anyone noticing from where the tree has been plundered.

Another fascinating plant is a scented, pink flowered, rhododendron, which has a distinctly expensive, after-shave smell. Quite pleasant, when you got used to it! Best of all though, is a

Craig Llyn blends into the beautiful Border scenery all around.

Pieris, rhododendron and the purple foliage of an acer at Craig Llyn.

medium sized rhododendron with a mauve-pink flower and scented *leaves*. Most unusual, and a plant I have never seen or read about before.

A dry stone wall and loose plantings of conifers and deciduous forest trees separate the garden from the surrounding countryside, with rougher areas allowed to go their own wild way close to the periphery. Spaces have been left between the trees however, so that the River Wye – which one can constantly hear – is glimpsed from the house and from various viewing points around the garden. Typical of the country around, and also fitting well into the ethos of the garden, are the self-seeding Welsh poppies in orange and yellow, as well as the banks of heather which give colour when the rhododendrons are out of season. The owner pays tribute to the heather, as the only plant she finds slug, mole and rabbit proof.

Craig Llyn is not an easy garden to look after, being both labour intensive and on a difficult, precipitous site, but it repays the owner for all her efforts with scent, sound and colour throughout the year.

Cricklewood Cottage - Shropshire

Medium sized cottage garden bordered by a river, full of interesting plants. Open under the National Gardens Scheme (see Yellow Book).

The gardening bug tends to strike late, with the onset of middle age – just look around your local gardening centre if you don't believe me – but the occupants of Cricklewood Cottage have obviously sustained an early infection! This garden however, could not be more traditional, being a catholic mixture of all that is best in the old-fashioned style of cottage garden. The general ambience is greatly helped by the white painted, low slung house, which was once a cottage smallholding with a thriving dairy. The old dairy steps still lead down the bank close to the back door, ending actually in Minsterley Brook, where dairymaids once drew the abundant supplies of water needed for their work. The male half of the gardening partnership saw a step one day, kept excavating, and discovered the whole flight intact.

The garden is long and narrow, angled from north to south, and bordered on one side by the aforementioned brook running in a deep hollow, and on the other, by a moderately busy road. Trees and the house cushion the garden against intrusive traffic noise however, so that you are much more aware of the music of the river, than the occasional roar of a diesel engine. The opposite bank of the river is heavily wooded, providing an interesting background of deep shade, underplanted with wild garlic.

The owners of Cricklewood began on one side of their plot five or six years ago, and worked slowly to the other. They are now terracing downwards towards the river, all stone from a demolished barn on site being finished, actually using large boulders dug from the bed of the brook. The river flash floods only part of the way up this bank – so all planting is safe – runs cool and clear with trout lurking in its depths, and includes a small, natural waterfall, I am green with envy, and cannot imagine anything more delightful than sitting in the newly dug out sunken terrace area, which commands a view of the waterfall as well as distant woods and hills. A new path to the water is also being excavated, which will enable you to walk along right beside the river to a flat stone 'beach' at the furthest end of the garden.

Up above, close to the house, old-fashioned flowers flourish in the well drained, but moisture retentive soil. When we visited in late May, the aquilegias were at their best, enjoying the wet, cool, season. Not only the common forms are planted, I noted 'Nora Barlow' in pink, cream, green and white; also *Aquilegia vulgaris clematiflora*, in pink, which has a very flat, open flower, as its name implies. *A.vulgaris*, with variegated foliage grows well, as does the lovely pure white. Pride of place for me, however went, to an extraordinary double form, in what I can only describe as a dark raspberry colour – alizarin crimson with just a touch of white.

There is an outstanding collection of aquilegia at Cricklewood Cottage.

Hardy geraniums are also a feature at Cricklewood, as is the mingling of herbs and flowers in most beds. *Geranium thurstonianum*, deserves a special mention here, with its spiky, pink shaded to mauve flowers, as it is rarely met with, and the owners state that it really does bloom all summer.

The other end of the garden, lately planted, is much wetter and shadier. Here, many old conifers have been removed to create more light, and moisture lovers like Meadowsweet planted. It is a natural, unfussy part of the garden, but a mostly cream, white and yellow colour scheme has been followed to complement the cool, damp shade. This is a new garden, but already a pleasure to visit, and can only improve with age.

A cleverly sited pool at Diamond Cottage draws the eye back into the garden in spite of the panoramic view all around.

Diamond Cottage - Powys

A medium sized, hilly garden, created since 1988, high up on the north side of a mountain. Open under the National Gardens Scheme (see Yellow Book).

The owners of Diamond Cottage bought the property in 1980 as a holiday home, and then liked living there so much they decided to make it permanent. The directions given to us when we visited, were to keep on going up. And, when you eventually arrive at the cottage, seven hundred feet above sea level, nestling against the hillside, you can understand at once why the owners never wanted to leave. Mile after mile of glorious scenery, right to the far away Berwyn Hills, stretches out before you. Closer at hand, but still below the garden, the wooded Breidden Hills alongside the main road, look oddly small from the cottages vantage point. The view is even more spectacular right at the top of the mountain, but, from a gardeners point of view, the hill behind provides welcome shelter.

With all the 'borrowed' scenery, one finds oneself constantly tempted to look out of the garden, but a cleverly sited pond, close to the house, helps draw the eye back inwards. Steps up from the cottage lead to a steeply sloping lawn with island beds containing hardy herbaceous plants, and tough, wind and frost resistant shrubs. This lawn, and the beds, were created gradually over the last six or seven years with no particular plan, but exhibiting a sure eye for the unusual and beautiful. I admired *Stipa gigantea*, a very good, bronze coloured grass, with light, airy plumes; much better suited to the terrain, and far more wind proof than Pampas grass, while almost equally eye catching. Another superb plant, quite new to me, is a dwarf, white daisy with the finest of fimbriated petals. I grow the tall form, but the plant at Diamond Cottage has all the advantages of a dwarf, compact, habit of growth.

There are few trees in this part of the garden, but as you mount the ridge to the top of the knoll, a surprise awaits you. The path, still producing head turning views, plunges downwards into an unsuspected dell, with a trickling stream heard from a distance but not seen; native oak, ash and sycamore and a great bank on the right, planted up recently with yet more herbaceous perennials. The owners eventual aim is to have no earth showing on the bank, and the fertile, moist, clay soil, is already disappearing fast.

The worst problem in this part of the garden is wild bracken, beautiful in small quantities, but a dreadful weed to eradicate. Strong weedkiller and persistence are winning the day, but odd clumps still crop up, even after three years. Surprisingly on such a steep slope, drainage is far from perfect, the garden frequently being waterlogged in the winter time. To assist the process, a natural spring at the top of the hill has been redirected underneath to appear below the bank and falls in a series of pools to the river running in the dell. The pools are unexploited as yet, but I cannot believe such a promising habitat will remain unplanted for long.

As you move away from the main garden, the plants get wilder and the paths steeper. The garden is only 1.7 acres, but the hilly nature of the ground means that it appears much larger. Out of sight of the house, bluebells, primroses, and when we visited in August, great sweeps of the delicate cranesbill, Herb Robert, were in control while silver birch provide just the light shade our native wild primrose needs. It is worth remembering, if you are ever tempted to dig up wild primrose plants, that they will not thrive in bare soil, or in a hot, dry position. Better to leave them where they are, unless you can provide the perfect conditions of Diamond Cottage.

Dinben Isaf - Denbighshire

A medium sized, hilly garden, close up against the Eglwyseg Mountains near Llangollen. Open occasionally for local charities.

Dinben Isaf is a garden made with a distinct purpose – to provide a wide range of flowers and foliage for the staging of the annual Llangollen Eisteddfod. Many people have a border for cut flowers, Dinben Isaf is a whole garden for cutting. Appropriately, it is only a little way up the valley from the Eisteddfod field, the limestone crags of the Eglwyseg range overhanging the garden, with just an intervening wood.

The stone built, low, Welsh farmhouse and its accompanying farm buildings, nestle in a hollow and back against the mountain, while the garden spreads out and upwards alongside. An even older Welsh longhouse, now abandoned to sheep, provides shelter and beautifully weathered walls for climbers, while from the highest part of the garden, Dinas Bran Castle seems only a stones throw away, and almost on the same level.

The owners and creators of Dinben Isaf have lived there for forty years, the garden growing with their interest. It houses an extraordinary exotic and unusual collection of plants, chiefly herbaceous perennials laid out in the most natural manner. For me, the greatest charm of the garden is the way such a sophisticated group of flowers, shrubs and trees, can look so at home on a wild Welsh mountain side. There is no sense of artificiality. It is hard to tell where the garden ends and the woods begin, especially in the spring-time, when cultivated bulbs and wild flowers mingle.

The rare and difficult *Clematis florida bicolor* 'Sieboldii', like some tropical Passion flower, looks perfectly at home on the woodshed door for example. While the yard near the back door, is decorated with over a dozen well planted alpine troughs. Most are of natural materials; all seem to have grown there.

The owner of Dinben Isaf gardens on almost the same level as Dinas Bran Castle.

The garden's greatest assets, apart from the wonderful scenery all around, are the rocky outcrops which add such a variety of terrain, and give scope for really exciting planting. One huge stoney mound, with foxgloves, wild pennywort in full flower, *Sedum acre* and stonecrop, is a perfect natural rock garden. The top, crowned by three twisted oaks, is like a full sized bonsai group, the whole set off by a small statue seen against the light at the summit.

With the emphasis on cutting, many tall, statuesque flowers are favoured, such as delphiniums; monkshood, also in shades of blue; campanulas in great variety, and foxgloves – the latter in pink and white. There are many double poppies in the garden to provide splashes of shocking pink, red and mauve, while euphorbias, especially the acid green, annual form, makes a perfect, cool, background, both in the garden and a vase.

There are many roses of course, mostly ramblers and climbers on the abundant walls, but H.T. roses also have a place, mixed in with other shrubs. Other unusual plants noted include yellow phygelius the tall Plume Poppy, *Macleaya cordata*, with its superb foliage, and hollyhocks in the most subtle colours imaginable.

Most of the trees are native species, but an old dual purpose apple called, the Druid, flourishes. It is the only one the owners have ever succeeded with at their altitude. Steep, Swiss style paths wind upwards towards the cool woods, where a simple wooden seat enables you to sit surrounded by the scents of the woodland and absorb the garden, the view, the castle, and the mountains on all sides.

The Dingle Garden and Nursery - Powys

A large garden on a sloping site, with fine natural lake and a magnificent collection of shrubs and herbaceous perennials. Open daily throughout the year, except Tuesday. Tel: (01938) 555145

It was never easy to find The Dingle, but nowadays the path is worn smooth by the many visitors to the excellent nursery alongside this exciting garden. It is exciting because the owner gardens dangerously, flirting with a number of plants which are on the borderline of hardiness. The terrain is precipitous, but unlike the formal terraces of Powis Castle Gardens – just over the hill – the garden at The Dingle is allowed to descend in a natural slope, the paths hairpin bends in gravel and logs, to a sheet of water at the bottom something between a lake and a pond,

The whole garden is beautiful, in both layout and situation, but the real *raison d'etre* of The Dingle, are the plants. You can find treasures at any time of the year, revelling in the sunny, south-west slope, and picking out just a few is no easy task.

First to catch your eye are the trees. As the garden is relatively new, of no great age, but chosen with a plantwoman's eye. The *Eucalyptus niphophila* close to the side of the pond, is an example of a tree on the tender side away from the south and west; but well worth trying for its exceptionally beautiful bark, which is striated in shades of grey and white with an occasional blue/grey tinge. The leaves are sickle-shaped, and also blue-grey, with the characteristic, pungent smell of eucalyptus. Eucalyptus come from Australia but vary in their ability to thrive in our climate. Seed is the preferred method of propagation, and it apparently varies in hardyness according to where collected in Australia. Choose young plants (which establish better) and a sheltered site, then pray for a few mild winters until the trees are growing strongly. If cut by severe weather, most can be pruned hard and will sprout again from the base. It was at The Dingle, I first saw *Betula utilis var.jacquemontii*, the Himalayan birch, a wonderfully elegant small tree, with bright, white, bark. The leaves also turn clear yellow in the autumn, prolonging its season.

Another large shrub whose flowers are incidental, is the pieris. There is a well grown group of *Pieris* 'Forest Flame', half way down the slope, sheltered by surrounding trees and bushes from cold winds, and showing their appreciation by the size and vigour of their brilliant red leaves. Some foliage was already fading to pink, and as the season progresses, it passes through a yellow/green stage, before becoming all green. There are white, scented, tassels of flowers, but the leaves are the main reason for growing this beautiful shrub-which only thrives in acid soil incidentally.

Eucalyptus niphophila. *Tender, but with such superb bark, well worth trying in a sheltered spot.*

39

Looking across the lake to the steep bank at The Dingle.

The sculptured forms and interesting colours of many mature, but dwarf conifers give the garden great substance, even in the depths of winter. The steep bank seems to suit the habit of growth of many of the prostrate kinds, especially when they hang over miniature cliffs, showing off the contrast between their mature and young foliage like the pieris, though in more subtle shades of green, blue and yellow.

Many choice plants such as Japanese acers and weeping copper beech, are used singly to mark corners where paths make acute angles on the steep slope. In other areas though, one cannot help but guess that the owner of the garden has instant access to a nursery, as many of the most rare and expensive plants are found in large groups.

I knew the garden twenty years ago when it consisted mainly of a bumpy lawn at the rear of the house, and some raised beds, but even then, the wide borders were filled with treasures. The owner has lived in the same property for over fifty years, and it shows in the detailed knowledge of the gardens many microclimates, from steep-dry bank, to woody shade and wet land near the lake. It now covers several acres, but a further area is being cleared for planting. At The Dingle though, more really does mean better.

Dolwen - Powys

A medium sized, hilly garden, planned around a series of ponds with interesting plants and breathtaking views, open every Friday from the beginning of May to the end of September. Tel: (01692) 91780411.

You reach Dolwen by way of a narrow and precipitous lane. So narrow, that red campion, ferns and scabious brush the sides of the car, so steep that ones heart is in ones mouth in case another car is attempting the journey in the opposite direction, It is only at the top that you learn with relief there is another way down.

Naturally, the garden, set squarely in the rolling Welsh hills near one of the wonders of Wales – a 250 ft waterfall – is on a steep slope. Unusually, the house is at the bottom of the hill, and seems to play little part in the general design of the garden: though it is perfectly in keeping–a typical, low, white painted cottage. The garden grew slowly over many years, the owner telling me that she likes to begin a major project every autumn.

The area close to the house and sited well above it, so that one looks down on the roof and walls, contains a small lawn, a vegetable garden, and conservatory. The really fascinating part however, is a lightly shaded, damp garden, not quite a bog garden proper, but full of plants which appreciate moisture without actually getting their feet wet. The water comes from a delightful stream flowing in a stony hollow. Crossing points are mostly of simple slabs of slate, but I noticed one wooden bridge, and a miniature arch of stone further up the valley. Foliage shape and colour, as much as flowers, makes this damp, shady garden outstandingly beautiful throughout the year. Primula are of course found in abundance, but ranunculus, meconopsis, ligularia, hosta, and *Caltha palustris*, Marsh marigold, also thrive. It was interesting to see hosta in many forms, grown in much the same way they might in the wild. That is, in a vertical position hanging close to falling water, so that their leaves are permanently misted. Judging from their size and vigour, both the hosta and ferns at Dolwen like this treatment.

Twelve years ago, the owner acquired a further area of mountain above her house, through which her stream flowed. Undaunted by the rocky terrain, she hired a J.C.B., and set about damming and digging, creating a chain of three large ponds. Many massive rocks came out of the holes, some interesting in shape and texture, and these have been used to advantage in this part of the garden. Massed, exploited as seats, or simply piled in an informal rock garden, they fit perfectly

Architectural plants make a definitive state-ment around one of the ponds at Dolwen.

into the garden landscape. One, placed on end and strategically sited next to the lowest and largest pool, is the resting place of a bronze eagle, who stares fiercely at the ducks disturbing its calm water.

The planting around the three pools is also biased towards good foliage shape. Large architectural plants such as gunnera, rodgersia, Solomon's seal, spiky variegated Iris, and once again, large forms of hosta, being the mainstay.

I must mention the many beautiful and well placed pieces of original sculpture in the garden, and declare an interest as an art trained connoisseur myself. It is no easy task to find the 'right' piece at a reasonable price, but the owner of Dolwen has succeeded many times. Treasures range from a weathered stone Japaese lantern, to several contemporary bronzes. This is yet another wonderful, Border garden, where the creator seeks to adapt to the surroundings, and go with the genius of the place, rather than impose her will upon it.

Erddig Park - Wrexham

A large, eighteenth century, formal garden, recently restored to its former glory. Owned by the National Trust and open frequently in season. Also open for the National Gardens Scheme (see Yellow Book).

The garden at Erddig is a mixture of the formal-clipped foliage; straight, sharp angled paths-and the utilitarian apples and pears on walls and grown in the grass. Fruit and flowers combined, in what, in a smaller garden, could almost be described as cottage style. I think this reflects the idiosyncratic temperament of its past owners, the Yorkes, who were also a curious combination of the homely country squire, living in a large sophisticated house filled with exotic furniture.

It is hard to separate the garden from the surrounding parkland, though the former is enclosed by a high wall, The wonderful trees of the Home woods press in all around. They are mostly composed of native beech, oak and yew, but further out in the park several enormous old conifers, including the Monkey puzzle, *Araucaria araucana*, still survive from original plantings, and I was delighted to see them being augmented with younger specimens.

I knew Erddig well as a child, all present views therefore are seen through a filter of the past. It is hard to look at the long canal, now so beautifully restored with the magnificent, eighteenth century iron gate and railings rescued from nearby Stansty Park and re-erected at the far end, without picturing it filled with mud, tadpoles and rotting logs. Close to the house, there is now an immaculate lawn and colourful flower beds around the stalagmite fountains to which Philip Yorke, the last Squire of Erddig, once tethered the goat he referred to as his 'lawn mower'. Some

Georgian symmetry at Erddig.

of the magic does depart when the family leave and the National Trust take over, but I am enough of a realist to know that Erddig had to be restored, or it was doomed.

The great, walled garden was laid out between 1718 and 1733, in what was, at the time, reckoned a somewhat old-fashioned style. The original concept included a bowling green, many summerhouses set into the walls (still intact) clipped yew hedges, and fruit trees, including such evocative varieties as, 'Orange Apricock' and 'Scarlett Newington Nectorn'. Great efforts have been made in the replanting scheme to include varieties contemporary with the original layout of the garden, and which otherwise might disappear from cultivation. The daffodils at the foot of many of the espalier apple trees are also older forms, including several varieties of rare, double, narcissus.

The shady north wall of the garden is host to the National Collection of ivies. The large variation in shape and size of leaf is well displayed, and, when you consider that most of the plain varieties have a variegated form, it can no longer be designated a dull plant.

The Yorkes did follow fashion in having the park 'improved', by William Emes, the landscape gardener. Streams were redirected and many trees planted, including the awe inspiring 'Cathedral', a double aisle of huge, smooth trunked beech, which gave the impression. of standing in the nave of a church, I say 'gave', as the great beeches were blown down in a storm some years ago. Once again however, the National Trust have replaced them in the identical place. Emes was also responsible for the 'Cup-and-Saucer', a cylindrical waterfall running through a tunnel and working a ram pump, which gives mysterious thuds from deep underground.

Visitors to Erddig Park and garden, step back in time to the early Georgian era when it was created. A truly fascinating experience.

Gardeners Lodge - Wrexham

A small, well-stocked, cottage garden, close to Offa's Dyke, and with an interesting eighteenth-century church nearby. Open under the National Gardens Scheme (see Yellow Book).

Trevor Hall can be clearly viewed from the Ruabon to Llangollen road. Not so its appropriately named Gardeners Lodge, which nestles close against the woods surrounding the hall, with Offa's Dyke path running just outside the garden gate.

In spite of the name, the present owners found nothing in the garden when they moved in five years ago. As the slope of the garden is steep, with magnificent views over the Dee valley, the first priorities were terracing with stones found on the site, and the making of a gently sloping lawn complete with a sunny patio for sitting outside to admire the views. The new bridge carrying the Ruabon by-pass was just going up, and the owners of Gardeners Lodge were able to watch its progress from start to finish.

The planting is a cottage mixture of shrubs, perennials and annuals, the latter mostly temporary until the permanent planting gets underway. The cottage atmosphere is further helped by a gaggle of geese, whose honking at strangers is as good a warning as any watchdogs. Soon after they

Achillea filipendulina *'Gold Plate' and the pink rose New Dawn, set off by grey stone walls.*

moved into the house, the owners attended a closing down sale at a nearby large nursery. Many of the bargains acquired helped to furnish the garden for a song, but, as most had lost their lables, many of the plants in the garden turned out to be pleasant surprises. The lovely pale-pink rose on the greystone front of the cottage is known however, New Dawn, a quick grower, even on a north wall, with double, cupped flowers, and a strong fragrance.

The garden is packed with naturalized snowdrops and daffodils early in the year – as are the woods all around – but when we visited, all the typical cottage favourites such as *Alchemilla mollis, Sisyrinchium striatum*, Marigolds, lavender, Sweet William, and pansies were in full blow, all interspersed with self-sown candytuft.

Several shrubs have made great progress in only five years – especially two *Daphne mezereum* close to the back door for early scent, the red berries in July as pretty as the February purple flowers. Also potentilla, spiraea, and low, ground-cover roses. Back among the perennials, I admired the blue and white *Campanula persicifolia*, both colours grown together, and the great clumps of *Achillea filipendulina* 'Gold Plate', which makes wonderful dried bouquets if you can bear to cut them in full flower.

Visitors to the garden can also walk to Trevor church, which was once the private chapel of Trevor Hall, and is just up the path. Here, the grounds are heavilly wooded with yews and native beech, oak, and sycamore. The woods are filled with snowdrops and flowering rhododendron in the springtime, and the views again spectacular. From one point, the viaduct, Telford's aqueduct with canal barges passing over, as well as the vast, new bridge in the background can all be clearly seen. The church is no less interesting, with the original box pews still in place, plus pegs on one side only for 'gentlemens top hats'

The cool, deep woods and the Dee valley, are the 'borrowed scenery' which make this garden so fascinating. It was also wonderful to learn that Trevor Hall, a perfect Georgian house contemporary with the church and lodge, is now being sympathetically restored after many years of neglect.

Garth House - Powys

A large garden with azalea and rhododendron wood, interesting stream garden and fine views. Open under the National Gardens Scheme (see Yellow Book).

Garth House looks Victorian, but is in fact much older. It has interesting historical associations with Charles Wesley, brother of John Wesley the preacher. Charles, who was better known as a writer of hymns, married Sally Wynne who lived at Garth House, and wrote *Jesu Lover of my Soul*, in the spare bedroom there on one of his visits.

The house backs up against a deciduous wood on a gentle slope. From the front, one has beautiful views over a mountain range, while closer at hand, green fields slope down to the river. House and garden all face front like some stage set, the woods in their early growth showing a hundred different shades of green like some painted back drop.

The planting at Garth House is relatively modern. The Victorians filled the clearings in the woods with the then fashionable rhododendrons, which were just being discovered and brought back to Britain. They have grown to a venerable size, and provide a colourful display underplanted with ferns and bluebells. I was struck by how good the new growth of rhododendrons can look, enjoying the contrast between the brown, furry, tomentum underneath, and the vivid green, upright new leaves. There is no doubt in my mind that rhododendrons need a large area of green around them like the wood at Garth House to provide a foil for their strident colours. One must take great care the colours do not clash in a small or open garden, where the eye has no cool green respite.

The water garden at Garth House.

There are several gentle terraces at the front of the house, the first, a half circle of grass with a border of low, creeping plants. Dividing the gravel drive from a large level sweep of lawn, is a curious line of slate topped, stone 'battlements'. I suspect that they were once a balustrade, separating house from field, though the effect now is almost that of a castellated ha-ha. The lawn falls yet again in a series of turf banks to a small brook, running parallel with the larger river away across the fields.

Well planted herbaceous borders are sheltered by the balustraded wall, which provides a grey stone background also useful as a windbreak. A small, fast flowing rivulet is hidden from the house by the lie of the land, and one has no idea of the pleasures in store until you are almost upon it. A mown grass path winds along the river bank on the house side – in fact much use is made of mown grass paths throughout the garden – while the opposite bank has been planted up with, among others, dwarf rhododendrons and azaleas, deutzia, and a superb Japanese maple. Marsh marigold and filipendula grow almost in the water, while *Iris sibirica* covers a grassy bank. Fine groups of hosta and many kinds of wild flower flourish in the long grass. The plants are not particularly rare or difficult, but all are well chosen and beautifully in scale with each other and the garden as a whole. A delightful finishing touch is the simple wooden bridge and wrought iron gate leading to the meadow with the big river in the distance.

Glanwye - Powys

Large, azalea and rhododendron filled garden, with wild flower and woodland areas close to the River Wye. Open under the National Gardens Scheme (see Yellow Book).

Glanwye fits snugly into the landscape, in a superb setting overlooking the River Wye. A busy road separates it from the water, but I have driven past many times without realizing such a lovely garden hides just over the hill. The house, which is built of local, weathered stone, blends into the garden, which in turn fades seamlessly into the surrounding countryside. The trees are magnificent, two enormous wellingtonia and a huge Irish Yew dominating the ground close to the house. The steep, tree covered slope at the back of the garden is known in Border country by the wonderfully evocative title of 'hanging woods'. When we visited in early spring, the leafless birch lightly covering the lower slopes were shading primroses, wood anemones and celandine; later, carpets of bluebells take their place. An occasional large cherry, its blossom as white as the trunks of the birch, adds to the spring-like picture.

The hillside was levelled for the house (built as a simple hunting lodge for a large estate, but much added to over the years) but almost the whole of the garden is on a steep slope. A bank of pink and white heather, loosely interwoven with the lawn, clothes the hill closest to the house. It is an excellent choice of plant for this position, long flowering, trouble free, and making the mowing of such a difficult area unnecessary. I am not in general fond of heather, but here, in its proper place, close to its native hillside, it really comes into its own.

The only other really flat area in the whole garden, is an old tennis court, now surrounded by a clipped yew hedge and creating a tranquil, formal, empty green garden, which is a welcome contrast to the great masses of brightly coloured azalea and rhododendron close to it. This part of the garden comes to life in late May, when it lights up with

The azalia walk, its gaudy colours toned down by a background of dark green.

46

every conceivable tint of red, purple, orange, yellow, white and pink, plus all the subtle apricot, mauves and creams in between. Most of the hill to the front of the house is covered in these large leaved, hybid rhododendron and azalea, arranged in loose walks with grass paths between, or in island beds underplanted with easy, shade loving perennials. I noted Solomon's seal, hardy geranium, *Lamium galeobdolon*, pulmonaria, *Euphorbia robbiae*, and the dark red early shoots of herbaceous paeonia yet to come.

Early spring in the bluebell wood.

Some of these mentioned, while excellent ground-cover, are tremendous 'rompers', and should be used with caution. *Euphorbia robbiae* and the lamiums in particular, can take over a small plot, but in the right setting, with room to spread, and where mown grass or other barriers prevent them colonizing areas where choicer plants grow, they can be a great asset.

Some of the rhododendron in the island beds look almost as good out of flower, by virtue of their beautiful leaves, and characterful, twisted trunks and branches. I guessed that they are of great age, and probably contemporary with the house. Welsh houses are notoriously hard to date, as the builders did not follow fashion, but went their own way with the local materials. When it came to the garden however, the owners were swayed by outside infuences, and the whole aura at Glanwye is mid-Victorian, when the first rhododendron were being discovered and creating such a sensation in the United Kingdom.

Gregynog - Powys

A large garden with fine trees, specimen shrubs, rhododendron and azalea, surrounding a black and white house. Open under the National Gardens Scheme (see Yellow Book).

Appearances can be deceptive. The gardens at Gregynog look like a typical Victorian rhododendron and azalea plantation, surrounding a genuine black and white, Elizabethan house. In fact the house was largely rebuilt in the mid-nineteenth century in imitation of a typical, 'timber-framed', Border house – it is actually moulded and painted concrete, covering brick – while the main rhododendron planting dates from the early twentieth century. The whole estate, always heavily wooded, was once vast, over eighteen thousand acres, and the prolific William Emes once again had a hand in some early plans. It has now shrunk to seven hundred acres, which together with the house, was gifted to the University of Wales by its last owners, the Davies sisters, in 1960, and in whose capable hands it remains.

The unique battlemented yew hedge at Gregynog.

The front of the hall faces a sunken area crossed by an ivy-hung bridge leading to a dramatic bank of brilliantly coloured rhododendron, backed in turn by a deciduous wood, mostly of oak, but punctuated by huge conifers stretching high in the sky. They are mainly wellingtonia, whose flat, dense green cones, contrast with the rounded, warmer greens of the other trees. The slope of sunken grass, and the huge scale of the planting, makes this one of the most impressive shows of rhododendron and azalea I have ever seen

Standing on the long gravel drive which runs between the rhododendron and the wood, looking back at the house across the slope, a totally different picture emerges. An extraordinary golden yew hedge, low and long, with projecting buttresses, runs the whole length of the bank directly in front of the house. Once roses were planted within the spaces, but they could hardly have been more effective than the now empty gaps.

Away from the house is a Dell and Lily Pond Garden, which were developed by the Davies sisters into a bog garden containing many rare plants, and which is particularly beautiful in early spring when the candelabra primula are in flower. Ligularia with their green and bronze foliage and strong orange coloured flowers also make a fine show both in and out of bloom. One variety, *Ligularia* 'Gregynog Gold', is named after the estate.

Mention must also be made of the Great Wood, which contains trees over four hundred years old, and has been designated a Site of Special Scientific Interest. Planting continues, the university investing in yet more rhododendron, this time modern hybrids and species.

I also admired the choice of plants close to the house, the stark black and white, softened by ivy, clipped neatly window high, as well as magnolia, clematis, and wall shrubs such as *Garrya elliptica*, whose long tassels and evergreen foliage appreciate the warmth and shelter. Colour was

provided by *Genista lydia*, in shining yellow, whose neat habit of growth fitted it tidily beneath the windows without ever appearing to outgrow its space.

Four gardeners now undertake the work once carried out by twenty-four, but if the original owners and builders on the site, the Blayney family could return, I am sure they would heartily approve both its present looks and use.

Gregynog has a superb collection of rhododendron and azalias.

Hawarden Castle Garden - Flintshire

A large 'Victorian', garden/park, surrounding two castles, one Georgian, one a mediaeval ruin. The home of Prime Minister William Gladstone for 50 years. Open under the National Gardens Scheme (see Yellow Book).

When visiting the garden at Hawarden Castle, it is difficult to concentrate on trees and flowers, majestic and full of interest as they are, so steeped in history and of such architectural interest are the two castles on the site. For there is an old and a new Hawarden Castle, linked by the gardens. A 'modern' house – built in 1757 and castellated to Gothic splendour in 1809 – and a ruin dating from around 1277, dominating a mound to the north-west. The garden follows the architecture, a wild daffodil strewn hill surrounding the old castle, smooth lawns, paths and neat flower beds around the new.

Close to the house are three *Magnolia stellata*, usually recommended for a small garden, but although only planted in 1920, grown to a very large size. This magnolia is one of the easiest to grow, and is both early and beautiful.

The elaborate flower beds to the side of the house were removed in late Victorian times for economy, but a formal air still reigns, emphasized by a square garden

A bird's-eye-view of the 'new' castle, garden, and the Cheshire Plain from the old castle keep.

house with Gothic windows (described in Pevsner as a Tea House). There is a walk of formal steps and paths to one side of the steeply angled garden, dominated by a huge wellingtonia, *Sequoia gigantea*. This great tree is in the middle of an early eighteenth century, earth amphitheatre, which may have been designed by the prolific landscape gardener, William Emes. The walk leads eventually to Cut Throat Alley, a narrow, overhung path, which Prime Minister Gladstone had made to enable him to walk privately to church in the village.

The lawn slopes upwards towards the old castle on the other side of the garden, becoming wilder the further one gets from the house. Bird life abounds, jackdaws wheeling over the old castle, thrushes slipping under the rhododendron foliage, woodpeckers drilling all around, chiff-chaff, black-cap, and garden warblers; as well as mallard on the series of ponds near the rock garden.

The soil in the garden is typical, Cheshire, acid sand, which grows azaleas (of which there are a great variety) to perfection; massed with the rhododendron as rich green background in large island beds. Around the rock garden, which is sheltered by the lie of the land and a hedge of clipped yew, are choicer, early flowering, dwarf rhododendron; conifers and some of the small leaved hebes, which look not unlike dwarf conifers until one inspects them closely.

A deep ditch, once the ancient Chester to Conwy road, is spanned by a small foot bridge built in the eighteenth century. Passing over this, one climbs upwards through the ruined curtain wall, to the old castle's round keep. There are wonderful vistas at the top, giving a bird's-eye view of the whole garden, the Cheshire plain, and the Clwydian hills.

All tastes seem to be catered for in this garden, from the self-sown valerian and toadflax in the walls of the castle, to the more ordered formality close to the new house.

Hergest Croft Gardens - Herefordshire

A large and important garden of botanical interest, containing an outstanding collection of rare trees and shrubs. Open daily, Easter to the end of October. Tel: (01544) 230160.

Hergest Croft is very much a Border garden, the ancient barrier of Offa's Dyke running along the top of Hergest Ridge. The nearest centre of population is Kington, but many of the surrounding place names are uncompromisingly Welsh. For almost one hundred years, the house and grounds have been owned and gardened by three generations of the Banks family, most of whom have been keen and knowledgeable plant collectors. Introductions by the great plant hunters of the early twentieth-century are to be found throughout the gardens, some dating from their original expeditions and therefore the earliest plantings of these species in Britain, making the gardens of great botanical interest.

The grounds are large and fall naturally into several distinct areas, the more formal plantings close to the red brick, Edwardian house. One part, an old oak plantation known as the Park Wood,

A stunning spring combination of Fritillaria meleagris alba *and pink erythronium.*

can only be reached by crossing fields where sheep graze. There are a great many native wild flowers in the wood, but its glory are the huge rhododendron hybrids and rare trees. The benign microclimate, shade, and moist soil (there is an old irrigation pond in the wood) provides ideal conditions for the larger rhododendron all year round. I am not in general a lover of the large flowered rhododendron, but the light shade and all-pervading green of the Park Wood, mutes and diffuses the strong colours, making this part of the garden an absolute joy to visit in the spring. The

Some of the trees at Hergest are the earliest specimens planted in this country.

gaudy azaleas too, have a wood to themselves, but closer to the main garden, where once again the many beautiful trees tone down their bright colours.

Acers there are in plenty at Hergest. I do not want this to sound like a plant catalogue, but must mention *Acer palmatum* 'Senkaki', one of the best for glowing red autumn colour, and a huge *Acer shirasawanum aureum*. Close to the shrimp-pink *Acer pseudoplatanus* 'Brilliantissimum', at the side of the house, I found one of the most delightful plant associations I have ever seen, *Fritillaria meleagris alba*, growing in quantity with the pink form of *Erythronium dens-canis* in fine grass. Totally original, and outstandingly beautiful in early spring.

A favourite part of the garden for me, is the old croquet lawn, which is an oasis of cool green and yellow shades. It is surrounded by a high, clipped yew hedge, the entrances marked by golden Irish Yews. In the summer, pots of lilies are used to give added interest. Notable trees in this area, include *Halesia carolina*, the snowdrop tree, which has unusual white, bell-shaped flowers in June. Often out at the same time, are a group of spectacular –and very old tree peonies, while earlier in the year, a pink *Magnolia cambelli* decorates the area, if not cut by April frosts.

Although Hergest Croft is best known for its magnificent trees and rhododendrons, another fascinating part of the garden – often overlooked by visitors – is the kitchen garden and orchard. It is much more open than the main garden, and has both well drained soil and a southerly aspect. Bulbs and herbaceous perennials do well, many rare and desirable, all interesting and well grown. It was here, that I first became acquainted with *Clematis recta* 'Purpurea', now, needless to say, in my own garden. Always get the purple leaved form which is far superior to seed raised, green specimens, and grow through a strong bush for support, such as lilac or philadelphus. It will reward you with masses of small, white flowers, and can be cut to the ground in the autumn.

There are also fine groups of *Romneya coulteri,* the Californian tree poppy, with large, white, tissue-paper flowers. This is one of those odd plants which is extremely difficult to get going, but once it settles, tends to take over the garden. There is much replanting in this area, including apples and a collection of walnuts, as well as a new bed of old roses.

One returns however to the main garden, where the original trees have now grown to full maturity and in autumn especially, are nothing less than breathtaking. In spite of the glorious tints from the acers however, I still think early spring is the best time at Hergest Croft, though any day in the year, from January to December brings nothing but pleasure from this wonderful garden.

Hodnet Hall Gardens - Shropshire

Over sixty acres of woods, water gardens, choice shrubs and herbaceous perennials. Open daily from April to September inclusive Tel: (01630) 084202.

It is inevitable that every tiller of the soil has favourite gardens whose layout and choice of plants they copy, or even aspire to emulate in full. Hodnet is one of my guide gardens. I think that your own plot and the garden of your choice has to have something in common; my garden is woody – Hodnet has an unrivalled collection of trees. The general ambiance at Hodnet combines meticulous maintenance with an enviable, unstudied air, which I like to think visitors also enjoy at Erway. Alas, I have only one acre, while Hodnet has sixty, to say nothing of a wonderful chain of natural lakes, dug in the 1920s from an unpromising bog in the valley below the house.

This series of lakes forms the backbone of the entire estate, with most water and damp loving plants hardy in the British Isles represented in this part of the garden. Indeed, because of the generally benign influence of the ponds (they rarely freeze over, and are often covered by a warming mist) shrubs and herbaceous perennials not usually attempted away from the south and west are also planted close by. Perhaps the most striking of these is *Gunnera manicata,* with some of the largest leaves (five feet across) of any plant able to grow in Britain. It also sports strange, orange-brown seed heads, and needs a mulch of its own leaves to see it through a cold winter. Astilbes in large colour blocks are also a feature, as are the massed plantings of candelabra primula, which have self-seeded in great numbers to make a medley of tints in early May. Some of the best named varieties are *Primula japonica* 'Miller's Crimson', and *P.j.* 'Postford White', while the vivid orange of *P.bulleyana* stands out against the countless shades of green. Candelabra primroses will grow in a damp border in moisture retentive soil, but never look as luxuriant as when their feet are deep in soft mud. Having just acquired some new American hybrids however, I can vouch for their survival with just a little shade and a modicum of watering in a hot summer.

Hodnet is a garden planned to provide interest in every season, and its original creator (the father of the present owner) has succeeded famously. Daffodils begin the year, planted in a

The main garden at Hodnet is planned around a chain of natural lakes.

naturalistic manner in the grass around the lakes; but the chief delight for me at this time are the superb collection of shrubs. Azaleas and rhododendrons revel in the ample moisture and acid loam, but it is the large, mature magnolias, ranging from the well known soulangeana and stellata, to the rare and unusual virginiana, sinensis and obovata (syn.hypoleuca), which always take my eye. Not to be missed, are the *Trillium erectum*, and *T.grandiflorum*, growing en masse in the light shade of high trees, or enjoying the cool, moist soil close to the water, So often one sees just a few of these delightful plants, but a large group is a rarely experienced, and quite unforgettable pleasure.

Hodnet Hall, a red-brick Victorian house, stands at the top of a steep slope overlooking the water garden. From the top terrace there is a panoramic view south of the Shropshire countryside all around, as well as a fascinating, seventeenth-century dovecote. Other notable buildings are a beautifully restored tithe barn, and the half-timbered tea rooms, built on the site of the original sixteenth-century Hall.

In high summer, when paradoxically, most gardens are tired and most people wish to visit, Hodnet really comes into its own. Its mature trees provide a background for a wonderful collection of hydrangeas, ranging from sargentiana, so difficult without moisture and just the correct amount of shade, to *H.aspera villosa*; mariesii; and the easier *H.paniculata* 'Grandiflora', which will stand more sun. Herbaceous perennials in full bloom include agapanthus, *Gentiana asclepiadea*, hardy geranium, and many late flowering roses.

With such a number of rare trees and shrubs, autumn is perhaps the best season of all at Hodnet. There are many exciting acers, which rival the azaleas in the brilliance of their late colour. The most outstanding is *Acer palmatum* 'Osakazuki', not rare, but never in my opinion

53

bettered for the vibrancy of its red leaves. Berberis, cotoneaster, and sorbus, provide berries in white, yellow, pink and red, while *Callicarpa bodinieri*, has the most extraordinary mauve-coloured berries, like groups of tiny beads.

I can only suggest that you pay several visits in all seasons, otherwise you are sure to miss something wonderful in this superlative, all year round garden.

Kyre Park Shrubbery - Worcestershire

A large, landscape garden, with interesting architectural features, laid out in 1754, now in the process of restoration. Open April to October, Friday, Saturday, Sunday and Monday.
Tel: (01885) 410282

Kyre Park Shrubbery is a garden waiting to be discovered. Like the Lost Gardens of Heligan in Cornwall, it has lain hidden under a covering of leafmould and soil for many years. Now, it has fallen into loving hands and a programme of rehabilitation is under way.

The landscaped park covers twenty-nine acres (it was once much more) and is composed of great trees, silted up lakes in the process of being dug out, and a variety of typical eighteenth century features, including waterfalls, rapids, a ruin, a belvedere (viewing point), bridges, and numerous picturesque views, the design of which may – or may not – be by Capability Brown. At the moment, the chief delights are the wonderful trees, and the expanse of open water near the house, the latter covered in a thriving collection of water-lilies. Our native yellow, *Nuphar lutea*, or Brandy bottle, as well as more sophisticated pale yellows, pure whites, and a superb, huge white water-lily with pale-pink outer petals. All these must be very hardy and tough to have survived such neglect over the years.

In the park proper, I particularly admired a Fern-leaved beech, *Fagus heterophylla*, and a large Cedar of Lebanon, unusually, surrounded by other trees quite deep in the wood. There are many magnificent yews most 'only' a few hundred years old, but one famous giant, often measured in the past and frequently mentioned in old books on the area, is known as 'The Parted Yew'. It is almost certainly a thousand years old, and is contemporary with the Norman building which once occupied the site of the present house. An air of mystery and romance pervades this part of the wood, which, although now approachable by a new gravelled path – 80 tons of gravel were used all around the lakes – I am sure will retain its sense of history and intrigue.

Acers at Kyre Park make a golden carpet on the croquet lawn steps.

54

There are enormous badger sets close to the yew, which create problems when planting. The new owner of Kyre Park is a fern specialist, the woods, water and general aspect being perfect for his collection of hardy ferns. Badger paths, sets and habits must be studied first however, before precious plants can be laid out. Badgers and newly planted, delicate ferns do *not* mix.

The domestic buildings on the site have a complicated history. First a castle, the remains of which form the shell of the Georgian house built in 1754, the park being laid out at roughly the same time. There are interesting doors and superb Venetian windows still surviving in the main house, although the middle portion was altered completely in the twentieth-century. There is a vast tithe barn built in 1618, and, best of all, a circular, fourteenth-century Norman dovecot,

The 'Parted Yew', one of the oldest in the country, in the wood at Kyre Park.

occupying a focal point at the end of a sunken lawn. It was moved to its present site in 1754, but could hardly look better, surrounded by perfectly placed trees and with a background of typical, lightly wooded, hilly, Border scenery.

Kyre Park is gardening on a grand scale, with trees where you or I would use herbaceous plants, but the owners do intend to add interest, mostly with rarer, exotic trees such as magnolia, and the disbursement of the many ferns brought from their previous garden. They are of course, only at the beginning of their great adventure, but already there is much to see and admire, not least the collection of ferns in the nursery, many of which are for sale (the owner is a Gold Medal winner at Chelsea). It is going to be fascinating to see the garden emerge from its cocoon over the forthcoming years.

Lightwood - Clwyd

A charming cottage garden, with interesting, separate wilder area, and paved herb terrace. Not open to the public.

The approach to Lightwood is down a narrow lane. Hints that you are getting close come from waves of fluffy green *Alchemilla mollis* and glimpses of unusual trees above a simple wooden fence. The fence hides Lightwood garden Part Two, and is entered by a gate on the other side of the lane from the garden surrounding the house.

Whereas the main garden tends to be formal and flowery, the 'extra' garden across the lane is steeply sloping and of an altogether wilder nature. It still contains treasures however. My favourite is a huge *Metasequoia glyptostroboides*, growing deep in the ditch. This deciduous conifer, with beautiful airy foliage, colours well in the autumn and obviously enjoys a damp

The delightful new herb garden at Lightwood.

position. The owners' favourites include a well shaped conifer with light flimsy leaves in a most unusual pale yellow, grown from a cutting and of unknown variety, as well as a tortured apple tree supported by sleepers with the air of an old man sitting on a stool. In fact, old apple trees are found in both gardens at Lightwood, another in the main garden, with a double trunk, giving the impression of someone crossing their fingers 'for luck'

Lonicera hedges, square clipped, define a paved area close to the house which gives shelter to a number of tender plants not usually found out of doors in the chilly northern Borderlands. The owner failed with the notoriously difficult *Crinodendron hookerianum*, known and loved for its bright red lanterns, but has succeeded famously with *Hebe hulkeana*, the very best hebe for a sheltered site, a glowing yellow *Choisa ternata* 'Sundance' and a large *Bupleurum fruticosum* bush. The contrast between the dull green leaves and the dark yellow flowers of the latter, rather like bunches of pins pushed into a ball, make it one of my favourite shrubs. Camellias, *Abutilon vitifolium* and several 'just' hardy fuchsia, grow well against the conservatory wall.

The conservatory is the third important garden element at Lightwood. Not only does all the hard work of propagation go on inside, but the brick wall opposite the run of windows plays host to some exciting tender climbers. A large pink pelargonium has been trained upwards almost to the roof, and intertwines with a superb dark blue perennial convolvulus. The latter has the advantage of dying gracefully, dropping its dead blooms on the floor beneath instead of clinging to them. Also doing well is an exotic Passion flower, while vibrant red, old-fashioned geraniums in terracotta pots decorate every available surface.

Outside the conservatory doors, a recent innovation is a small herb garden. Herb gardens are very tricky to keep looking good right into full summer, most herbs having a tendency to grow long and leggy. At Lightwood however, they are confined to neat areas with brick paving and grey-stone slabs between. Staddle stones stand at each corner, with a sundial centrepiece and a full stop of three dwarf apple trees at the end. It all works beautifully, the exuberant spilling over of the lavender, lemon balm, parsley and golden marjoram, softening the hard paving.

The rest of the garden is laid out in simple style with one large island bed surrounded by lawn, and wide edging borders backed by country hedges dating from a time when the house was a farm. In late summer, when we visited, the yucca was in full flower and a wonderful sorbus tree with orange fruit the size of golf balls were just two treasures noted at once. I have never known the borders without something of interest, either in flower, foliage, bark or berry at any time of the year you care to pay a visit.

Lingen Nursery & Garden - Shropshire

An alpine and herbaceous nursery surrounded by a varied garden. Open February to October by appointment, also under the National Gardens Scheme, (see the Yellow Book).
Tel:(01544) 267720.

Lingen is primarily a specialist alpine nursery, but it also holds part of two National Collections – *Iris sibrica* and campanula. The latter were in their full glory when we visited in early July, though there are many more varieties of rare and unusual plants to admire in the two acres of garden surrounding the nursery.

I cannot pass by any campanula, never having found a single form I do not admire and covert

for my own garden. At Lingen, the first plant I saw was a particularly graceful, white, persicifolia, called the 'Cup and Saucer' form. It is very old, having been known since Elizabethan times. The shape is charming, but what makes it even more attractive, is the faint hint of green in the flower. A complete contrast, is *C.latiloba* 'Hidcote Amethyst', with showy, large, mauve/pink bells, clustered around stout stems.

As this is an alpine nursery, the dwarf campanulas are also well represented, the rarer forms in raised scree beds to give the special conditions they require, but many of the easy to grow varieties making great clumps in the main garden. I have always loved the white double campanula, 'Boule de Neige', but at Lingen I saw 'Fleur de Neige' for the first time-and learnt the difference; 'Fleur de Neige' has a tighter flower.

The main garden has few trees, to give the alpines and herbaceous plants the open, sunny conditions they require. The exception, is a single enormous yew, sheltering the foxglove *Digitalis parviflora*, a plant which can stand some shade. Although small, it is subtly spectacular, a pyramid of brown, tubular flowers, very closely packed on the stiff stem and sprouting from a base of narrow leaves. I liked the

A 'Cup and Saucer' campanula, one of the many at Lingen.

way this part of the garden was given substance by the dwarf conifers which provided an evergreen framework for the more amorphous herbaceous plants. *Juniperus communis* 'Compressa' is particularly successful, as are the whipcord hebes, which look at first glance not unlike small conifers and serve the same purpose. The paths are of small sized gravel, which is allowed to spread and merge with the border, giving ideal conditions for dianthus, of which there are also many forms. The dwarf hardy geraniums, such as 'Ballerina', pink with a black eye; and the compact sanguineum types in pink, white and magenta, also appreciate this treatment judging by the size and beauty of the clumps at Lingen.

To the left of the drive which leads into the nursery, a large earth mound has been converted into a rock garden ablaze with sunroses, the helianthemums. A glowing orange, fleshy pink, and a striking yellow ochre took my eye. I only grow the double forms, but after seeing the singles at Lingen, feel inclined to try them again, in spite of the flowers fading so swiftly in hot sun. Also on the mound, I made the acquaintance of a new diascia called 'Rupert Lambert', in a very different pink. All the diascias make a neat clump in well-drained soil, or will drape well on a raised bed. They flower all summer, and appear trouble free. 'Ruby Field' is the reddest; 'Salmon Supreme' the best apricot; while 'Lilac Bell', describes itself.

A new bed for large herbaceous perennials and shrubs is in the process of being planted up away from the main selling area of the nursery. It is already well established, because of the excellent growing conditions and moisture retentive soil. There are more campanula, as well as part of the *Iris sibrica* collection, but I was attracted to *Paeonia tenuifolia* with the finest, thread-like foliage in rich green, contrasting with brilliant, single, red flowers. Also the white form of epilobium which I grow myself. It runs, but mercifully does not seed. There is *Campanula triqueteum*, some superb penstemons – I could go on ad infinitum.

Pay a visit and see them all for yourself.

Llangedwyn Hall - Powys

Large, formal terraced gardens, laid out in the late 17th and early 18th century. Open under the National Gardens Scheme (see Yellow Book).

The grand terraced gardens at Llangedwyn Hall are a rare survival from the early eighteenth century, made especially important by the lack of interference to the original plan by later owners. Today, the only concession to the twentieth century is that the garden is planted in the most delightfully informal manner, with plants spilling over onto the gravel walks, and continuity of flowering assured not by bedding plants, but by the use of mixed borders, as well as both modern and old roses.

The gardens appear large and complicated, even when the historically important house they surround is taken into consideration. Once, they extended even further – a lower terrace for example, which was once a vegetable garden is now grazed by sheep, though the old retaining walls remain. A garden pavilion occupied a corner of a top terrace from where the house and surrounding hills could be viewed to advantage. Interestingly, a cellar under the ruined pavilion still survives beneath and behind the wall.

The house, 'modernised' in about 1718, dominates the garden. Fortunately, although much altered and reduced in the 1950s, it retains both its beauty and homogeneous relationship with the garden, as well as having many interesting features. These include an imposing classic style doorcase with columns, an outdoor clock (made in Whitchurch in 1857) as well as a fascinating painted sundial.

Any garden which has an abundance of beautiful, weathered brick walls, starts with a tremendous advantage, and the three great terraces at Llangedwyn, utilised to perfection for roses and many other climbers, make a superb background for the rest of the plantings. The grassed top terrace, also gives a totally new viewpoint, so that one sees the garden in a continually changing perspective as you walk around; first below, then above. A pure white rose is observed from ground level, looking up into the hanging flowers. Then, from the top terrace, one is able to admire the blooms in close-up, peeping over the low wall.

Llangedwyn is renowned for its magnificently unspoilt terraced garden.

The glorious setting of the house and gardens, with views over the unspoilt Tanat valley, can also best be appreciated from the top terrace. A new, open sided pavilion, has been built against the wall close to the house to sit and absorb the beauty all around. Outside, jet black urns show off both flowers and foliage, while long troughs are filled, one with pink geraniums, another with a glorious mixture of yellow helichrysum, yellow nasturtium, white daisies and yellow coreopsis.

The middle terrace is the widest, its centre taken up by a long lawn with two circular ponds. These boast fountains which spout three jets in imitation of the Prince of Wales feathers, and are worked from a small lake – the Briw – above the garden. The two, long, parallel herbaceous and shrub borders which flank this lawn, contain some lovely colour combinations. Lamb's Lugs in soft grey, pink roses, lavender and catmint are repeated along the lower border, giving continuity of scent and colour all summer. The other border, backed by a high wall, contains more variety. I noted in particular, *Rosa* 'Ballerina', set off by the purple *Berberis atropurpurea* 'Rose Glow', and Rosa Mundi, that perfect striped rose, again surrounded by Lamb's Lugs, Creeping Jenny, *Lysimachia nummularia* 'Aurea', in its choicer, yellow form: variegated *Euonymus fortunei* 'Silver Queen'; with pinks and the prostrate *Ceanothus repens* overhanging the path. Formality is further counteracted by the sight of toadflax in the wall – even a hardy fuchsia has found a foothold and been allowed to flourish.

The side of the house facing the road (which was once the front) is no less interesting. The lime avenue had to be replanted in the 1970s but is now well grown. It leads to a walled courtyard filled with roses in formal beds coloured apricot and dark pink, the weathered brick wall festooned with climbing roses. Two magnificent magnolias on either side enjoy the shelter of the walls; but more impressive still, the flight of semicircular steps leading up to the house, are flanked by two immense *Acer palmatum* with trunks worthy of oak trees and great, elephant's feet roots anchoring them to the ground. They dominate this part of the garden, the beauty of their plain green leaves setting off the showy roses.

Above the terraces the ground rises steeply with many individual trees, merging eventually into the mixed, deciduous, Warren Wood, and planted up with bulbs and azaleas to give spring interest. Even the more utilitarian areas of stable yard and service wing have their own beauty.

The opposite side of the rose garden wall for example, has pinky-grey brick set off by a narrow ribbon of *Bergenia cordifolia*.

This is a garden with every advantage of scenery, history and architecturally distinguished house; fully exploited, but not over gardened, to make a wonderful, uniform whole, at peace with its setting and itself.

Llysdinam - Powys

A large woodland, rhododendron and azalea garden, with fine views and adjoining herbaceous/ kitchen garden. Open under the National Gardens Scheme (see Yellow Book).

Architecture, landscape, and fascinating historical anecdotes come together at Llysdinam to create an intriguing picture. The house is basically eighteenth-century, but was much altered-indeed, partially demolished several decades ago, and now has a faintly Art Deco air, with simple, rounded, cream stucco walls and plain Georgian windows.

The landscape before the house, looking across the Wye valley to the hills beyond is breathtaking. The countryside around giving the impression of being encased in a time warp, though roads and cars are only too near at hand at the bottom of the hill. This is yet another Border house and garden having an association with the Victorian diarist Kilvert, a previous

A view from the old walled kitchen plot highlights the beautiful setting of house and garden.

owner employing him, and meriting several entries in the famous diary. Past owners of Llysdinam were not only interested in the management of their considerable property, but also – in the best Victorian style – took an amateur interest in photography, natural history, and the sciences. The University of Wales has a field centre locally, gifted to them by a previous owner, and continues a long tradition of nest box recording, thought to be the oldest continuous records in the country.

The garden was once formal, with bedding out plants in carefully manicured beds, as well as a vast rockery built some distance from the house for alpines; quite enough in its own right to occupy several gardeners full time. Nowadays, the garden reflects the countryside around, the beautiful mature trees on the lawns merging gradually into a sheltering wood. The area where woodland meets garden is delightful, with great mounds of *Hydrangea sargentiana* and Grandiflora, set off by yellow potentilla, Japanese acers, hebes and hostas.

A long shrub walk is bordered by a multitude of large azalea and rhododendron; flourishing, in spite of the poor shaly soil,

The house at Llysdinam has been much altered, but retains its architectural integrity.

cold winds and hot dry summer. Opposite, is a water garden with many complicated paths. The huge stands of Royal fern, *Osmunda regalis*, give some idea of the age of the garden. So often one sees interesting plants, but in tiny groups, at Llysdinam, big clumps of bamboo, Solomon's seal, pink filipendula, and daffodils as far as the eye can see in the spring time, give clues to when the garden was first established, and create the kinds of effects which can only come with time.

Crickets sing in the long grass close to the wood, but it is the buzzing of what sounds like a million bees which guides one through a wrought iron gate set in a yew hedge, to the enclosed vegetable garden with peach house and greenhouses. Once it would all have been given over to vegetables to feed the household, but a delightful pergola has been established in the centre of the garden to cover two bisecting paths, centring on a weathered sundial. On a hot day in late summer, the scents and sounds are delicious. Monkshood, achillea, hardy fuchsia, and heleniums were in full flower, with a vine shading the pergola. Other late favourites in a border on the house side of the yew hedge include, phlox, acanthus and potentilla, with Michaelmas daisies still to come for autumn interest.

But always, in spite of the pleasures of the garden, ones eye is drawn outwards to the spectacular views, unimpeded by the trees which cluster to the sides and rear of the house. The poet Wordsworth visited the house and must have been as inspired by the garden and its setting as visitors are today.

Maenllwyd Isaf - Powys

Three acre garden comprising both wilder and cultivated areas, surrounding a delightful sixteenth-century house. Open under the National Gardens Scheme (see Yellow Book).

'Dream cottage', is a hackneyed phrase, but it is difficult to think of any other epithet that describes Maenllwyd Isaf so well. Imagine a pink washed, timber-framed house, its walls hung with *Clematis armandii*, magnolia, and *Hydrangea petiolaris*, set in idyllic countryside, surrounded by peaceful, rolling hills, and filled with the sounds of birdsong and the far away music of the River Mule running through a wooded valley just below the house. Add to this a beautiful garden with mature trees, planted out in perfect sympathy with the house, and you have most people's idea of paradise.

When the owner removed from London in the fifties however, there was neither house nor garden, only a derelict shell with three and a half acres of field. The resultant garden and house (they fit together so well it is impossible to divorce one from another) are the culmination of forty years of love, imagination and hard work, which together with an impressive knowledge of plants and all their attendant whims, have produced a small masterpiece.

There was no plan, and after bulldozing and harrowing, the garden just grew out from the house gradually, the design based loosely on island beds of mixed shrub and herbaceous perennials. There are delightful surprises around every corner. A group of three raised beds made from great blocks of tufa and planted mostly with clump forming saxifraga. Two ancient, but

The picturesque cottage at Maenllwyd Isaf is very much part of the garden scene.

perfect Corinthian columns, the stone weathered as only age can, placed at the periphery of the garden where it meets the wood. A large rockery, constucted with stone rescued from a demolished building and all bought for £4 10s!

The garden is full of wonderful plants, collected over the years with an eye for the choice and original. A dierama for example, hanging over a pond, in the darkest possible pink, and a white *Crinum x powellii* 'Album', in the shelter of the cottage walls. There is the rare and expensive *Arisaema candidissimum*, with exquisitely striped pink and white, cowl-like spathes. Superb ferns enjoying the shade from the many well chosen trees – a Turkey oak, for the best, glowing red autumn colour; many cherries, including Tai-haku, with white flowers and again good for autumn tints as well as mature apples adding blossom, fruit, and characterful, gnarled trunks to the over-all garden picture. On the edges, the woodland takes over, with native trees such as copper beech, oaks, sycamore and silver birch. Sorbus are pleached onto iron frames to the side of the brick paved drive to divide it from the garden, while outbuildings, as old and beautiful as the house, shelter the property on the other side.

The back of the house hides a steep descent into a magical, natural garden, passing through wild flowers and tall trees – now mostly alder, ash and hawthorn – until you arrive at a long, clear pool in a sunlit glade, before following the sound of water downwards again to the river. Cultivated ground-cover, vinca and pulmonaria, vie with the wild, Herb Robert and native ferns. Early in the year, bulbs are triumphant – bluebells versus daffodils.

There is a hint of formality close to the side of the house. Neatly clipped box hedges and stiff Junipers standing to attention either side of the path. Also beautiful, square planters, simply filled with low, grey and pink *Sedum spathulifolium*, and a challenging modern sculpture in pale grey concrete, backed by lush greenery. It represents a seed held firmly between a finger and thumb. I cannot think of a better way to sum up the whole spirit of the garden.

The Miller's House – Powys

A one and a half acre country garden, begun in 1988. Open under the National Gardens Scheme (see Yellow Book).

When the owners of The Millers House moved to Powys from Cheshire six years ago, the intention was to renovate the two derelict cottages on the site and make the surroundlng rough field into a garden. In the event, a modern house was built alongside the old cottages which became garages and a store shed – though one still retains its bread oven. The garden however, did gradually emerge from the field.

The front area is small and somewhat complicated, the aforementioned cottages making a barrier down one side and now beautified by climbers *Clematis montana*, roses, and honeysuckle, well set off by the whitewashed walls. There are many roses, as well as easy to grow herbaceous perennials clustered around a good focal point, a rebuilt well-head and pump.

There are gorgeous views on all sides of the house of mountains both near and far. The low rolling hills of Powys close to the rear garden, and far flung vistas of the distant Berwyns from the side of the house, where a hedge was especially lowered to enjoy the view to the full.

The back garden is large and simply laid out, in contrast to the front, consisting of a wide sweeping lawn falling away from the house with mixed borders, a pond, and a fruit garden. Two mature Crack willows, *Salix fragilis* remain, once part of an old boundry ditch. They have been pollarded over many years and the one closest to the house, which has a compact habit of growth and a wonderfully textured trunk, has a wooden bench built around it to provide a delightful sitting out place. A circle of hardy geranium, including Wargrave Pink and *Geranium pratense*, the latter similar to Johnson's Blue but with a finer leaf, make a circle around the seat. Very simple, but an inspired choice.

The garden had no definite plan, but grew gradually year by year. The curved mixed border along the top of the garden slopes upwards at the rear, giving a good view of all the plants. It was built on the old cottage dump, but the flowers seem to like the site. I was fascinated by the edging of alpine strawberries, very pretty and practical. Standing out in this border when we visited,

were the *Dianthus deltoides* in a very dark red; *Senecio greyi*; *Astrantia maxima* in pink; purple sage – an excellent foliage plant foil all summer; *Rosa rugosa*; with tree lupins and hard pruned buddleia in the background. The border ends, with all the magellanica group of hardy fuchsia, much the toughest, and prettiest, with their light, graceful stems and small flowers. *Fuchsia magellanica gracillis*, is red and purple with green leaves;*F.m.g.* 'Variegata', has lovely pinky grey-green foliage and similar

The perfect place to enjoy all the scents, sounds and sights at The Miller's House.

flowers; while *F.m.* 'Alba'. has green leaves and pinky-white flowers. All are excellent in all but the worst winters, and can be cut back like herbaceous perennials in the spring.

The pond was constructed of butyl, though the ground at The Millers House has a sub-soil of clay. I thought the pebble beach to help wildlife in and out a very good idea. Many interesting trees have been planted which have yet to mature, but a grove of eucalyptus have bounded ahead (if you want instant gardening, this is the tree for you!) *Eucalyptus gunnii* is generally thought to be the hardiest, but many forms are reliable, and will sprout six feet in as many summer months. In just six years, the garden at The Millers House is doing quite as well.

Monnington Court - Herefordshire

A five acre garden with large lake, laid out to provide a background for a collection of contemporary sculpture. Open under the National Gardens Scheme (see Yellow Book).

The garden at Monnington is dominated by house, church, water and sculpture. The other overwhelming impression for me was animal rather than vegetable. The owners of Monnington are passionately interested in the Morgan horse and breed them on the farm nearby; naturally, they figure prominently in the sculpture with which the garden is filled. Birds are represented by flotillas of ducks; peacocks, screaming at the swooping swallows and house martins, and two, dignified, but fierce black swans, very much in charge on the large lake. White doves circle overhead wherever you wander, and a cat licked its paws and no doubt its lips, watching from a downstairs window.

The sculpture is an integral part of the garden, which has been deliberately planned to set it off. There is a steel circle in the lake for example, wth water jets, and a low stone, yin-yan, oscillating piece close to the house which works by the movement of water. More realistic, are a circle of portrait heads on pillars, in a small, square, enclosed garden at the side of the house. They are set in grass, surrounding a paved circle with a sundial and herbs, and look very effective backed by a rose hung wall, a choisya, and a *Philadelphus coronarius* 'Aureus', the yellow leaved Orange blossom. Elsewhere, at the apex of an avenue (newly planted with copper beech) is a shallow cement pond with a circular marble slab and a tall metal abstract piece reflected in the still water. An interesting curved walkway at the other side of the lake, covered with *Clematis armandii* – an evergreen only for a warm spot-ends with an unusual sculpture that resembles nothing so much as a giant pear.

I was interested to see that the owners tended to choose sculptural trees for new plantings, including several well grown weeping forms of cedar, birch and pear.

The house, which forms an important part of the garden scene, is mainly an ancient Moot Hall completed in 1230, and it is apparently rare to find one so untouched and in such excellent condition. It was very much enlarged in the fourteen hundreds and during the seventeenth century, when three old cottages were incorporated into the building. A stone thrown from an upstairs window would easily reach the church, it is so close. Again, it is a beautiful building, as old as the house, built and endowed by past owners of Monnington Court. A short avenue of roses leads from the garden to the church door, echoing another famous avenue nearby, 'Monnington Walk'. This is one of the oldest tree lined walks in the country, over a mile long,

and mentioned by Kilvert the diarist who lived close by and often strolled under its Scots pines and yews. I also found an echo of the mediaeval carvings at Kilpeck Church – which is only a few miles away – in the superb oak door which has a lintel worked on in much the same, naive manner.

The windows on this side of the house look out to the lake, over a sloping bank with a sitting out place, and a series of low plantings with a blue-grey theme of *Santolina*

Proving that restraining the colour scheme to blue, grey and green need not be dull!

pinnata neapolitana and lavender, all neatly clipped. But ones eye is constantly drawn back to the church and house, the sense of history which pervades the whole place, mingling with the beautiful scenery bringlng an overwhelming feeling of tranquility to the visitor.

Ness Gardens - Cheshire

A large garden made up of many diverse areas giving a variety of growing conditions and containing a magnificent collection of plants. The gardens are open daily from 9 a.m. to sunset, except Christmas Day.

Many people might quarrel with the idea that Ness is a Border garden at all. But what better border than the Dee estuary? Ness sits on a south facing slope close to its flat sandy-banks, with superb views to the Clwydian Range of mountains across the water. The gardens are now in the hands of the University of Liverpool, but were first laid out by Mr. A. K. Bulley in the late nineteenth century, the owner of the famous firm of Bees Seeds. The site was originally part farm land and part common, so there is a long tradition, originated by Mr Bulley, and carried on by Liverpool University, of public access.

Set against any standard, Ness gardens are huge, (60 acres) and encompass many differing environments which give ideal conditions for a great variety of plants. It is perhaps best known for the spectacular rhododendrons and azaleas which revel in the acid, sandy loam and the relatively milder climate of the Wirral peninsula. Most of the rhododendron are grouped in a wide border backed by a pine wood which both shelters the early flowerers and makes a satisfying, dark green background. My particular favourites are the small-flowered blue or mauve varieties, such as *Rhododendron x* 'Blue Tit', and *R.augustinii*, but there is also a good selection of the now very popular *R.yunnanense* and *R.yakushimanum* types, the latter much planted because of its fine foliage and compact habit of growth, ideal for the modern small garden. Perhaps most beautiful of all, are the waxy, tubular flowers of *R.x* 'Lady Chamberlain', which unfortunately needs absolutely perfect conditions – it receives them at Ness – to do really well. Ness also boasts one of the largest plants of *Pieris formosa forrestii* 'Wakehurst' in the country, whose red early foliage is as bright as any flower. Towards the end of the border, huge upright Loderi rhododendron, make towers of pink and white in late April and May.

The heather garden at Ness, is now justly as famous as the rhododendrons. The rocky sandstone site provided the perfect, well-drained bank on which to lay out their comprehensive collection. I am not a fan of heathers *en masse*, but at Ness, their flatness is enlivened by the strong shapes of conifers, prostrate and tall, dwarf and mature, while the white trunks of birch, and the background of deciduous trees on the top of the slope completes the picture. There are also island beds of heathers close by, the vibrant reds and purples contrasted with the upward growth of tree heathers, the grey-green of santolina, and tufts of blue grass.

Ness is well known for its superbly sited heather garden.

There is a water garden at Ness, a rose garden, and a quite magnificent rock garden, at its best early in the year. The trees deserve a special mention, both for their variety and rarity. Ness is host to the National Collection of sorbus, and almost all the important forms are represented somewhere in the garden.

To pick out just a few favourite trees is almost impossible, but the eucryphia with its scented white blossom set against the darkest of holly-green leaves in August, is especially noteworthy. I adore the Monkey puzzle, *Araucaria araucana*, close by the herbaceous beds, because it is a fairly young specimen and clothed right down to the ground. So often this tree has a frost scarred trunk devoid of branches, and looks like a dust mop. Best of all, a superb variegated oak, *Qercus cerris* 'Variegata', quite unique, with its boldly splashed cream and green leaves.

Ness is even worth a visit in mid-winter, when the heated conservatory comes into its own. The musty, hot dampness, exotic foliage and flowers, makes for a strange but fascinating experience on a cold January day. There is a temperate house, as well as a true 'hot house' with orchids and a huge banana, complete (most years) with fruit. A new departure, is a dry desert house with large succulents and cactus, already a mecca for all those interested in these weird plants.

I have space only to mention the herb garden, native plant collection, as well as all the smaller gardens and interesting corners with which the gardens abound. I cannot leave out the wonderful double sided herbaceous border however. It is planned to give interest after the main shrub and bulb display ends in June, and contains – to mention only a fraction of the plants – large clumps of paeonia and pyrethrum for early colour, followed by iris and Sweet peas trained on posts. In the hot dry days of August, when most gardens are looking tired, salvias, Golden rod, crocosmias, early Michaelmas daisies, agapanthus, phlox, helenium, monarda, eryngium, *Aster x frikartii*, *Achillea filipendulina* 'Gold Plate', and the towering Pampas grass, are only just getting into their stride! If you are short of ideas for high summer, do come and admire the herbaceous border at Ness, you cannot fail to go away inspired.

A final thought, the larger the garden, usually, the less meticulous the maintenance, Ness is never less than perfect the whole year round.

⑦he Old ⑬arn - ⑥Wrexham

A delightful small garden, planned to provide colour, tranquillity, and a plentiful supply of vegetables and fruit. Not open to the public.

There are no problems with the vegetation at The Old Barn, shrubs, trees, vegetables and herbaceous perennials flourish in the well-drained, south-west facing shaly hillside. Livestock however, are another matter, with slugs, snails, rabbits, moles, mice and pheasants, enjoying the bounty from the garden just as much as the owner.

The garden is set in beautiful countryside with views over the valley of the River Dee, and only a stones throw from the impressive wrought iron gates which mark the entrance to Chirk Castle. It runs above and to the side of an old Welsh stone house, which, as its name suggests, was converted from a barn and stables. Woods, fields, and superb views make it a very pleasant place

Mediterranean colours on a hot summers day at The Old Barn.

to live, even if the animal population insist on sharing There is an excellent vegetable garden at The Old Barn, with great banks of visually interesting herbs separating it from the grass paths around: purple sage with blue flowers, rosemary, santolina and lavender. Fruit trees are also a feature in the whole garden; one, which looked much older than the rest, was in the garden when the owner bought the property, and bears three kinds of apple. It appears to be a very early form of family tree, with different fruit varieties grafted on, now of course very fashionable for the smaller garden.

Planting generally is informal, and mostly composed of mixed beds of small trees, shrubs and perennials. The hebes were outstanding when we visited in July. Great Orme in pink, and Marjorie – blue fading to white – looked particularly good, though a steep, rocky area, planted with carpeting alpines, contained some delightful dwarf hebes with just neat green leaves. The owner has wisely picked out only the most hardy of the genus, as the altitude he gardens at makes any tender forms too much of a gamble. Hebes are so easy from cuttings however, it is always worth while propagating them every year in case of a severe winter. Also growing on the rockery are some dwarf conifers which give shape when the garden is bare, though heavy snow can break the flatter branches down. Colour, in the heat of summer, came chiefly from low plantings of *Dianthus deltoides* 'Flashing Light'; heuchera; *Geranium sanguineum*, both the common purple and pink form, and a lovely double Sun rose – helianthemum – in dark red, possibly Firebird.

There are many potentillas in the garden, closely intertwined with the other shrubs to make wonderful, weed-proof beds. They have knit together so well in some places it is hard to tell where the potentillas end and the hebes begin!

The many good roses in the garden also deserve a mention. I was particularly impressed with a huge specimen of Paul's Himalayan Musk over a plum tree – a tower of scent and colour. Also a very good old single white rose, Pleine de Grace; New Dawn on an arch, and a beautiful hedge of rugosas. In fact roses and dry stone walls make up most of the gardens boundries, fitting in well with the natural, unforced air throughout. A seat at the top of the garden, enables the owner to sit and admire the whole when the days work is done.

Pen-y-Wern - Flintshire

A two and a half acre terraced, country-house garden incorporating interesting small gardens. Open under the National Gardens Scheme (see Yellow Book).

Some gardens are described as 'gardens within gardens' in the manner of Hidcote and Sissinghurst, when they contain little more than borders facing a variety of aspects and with differing micro-climates planted appropriately. Pen-y-Wern really merits the title.

It is a complicated garden surrounding an old manor farmhouse (there is a date stone from 1754) on many different levels and including most of the old farm buildings, Some of the latter have been demolished in the past, but the stone has been utilized to build high, castellated walls, hiding and sheltering the area to the rear of the house, so that a walk in the garden becomes a voyage of discovery. Where there are no walls, very high beech hedges cast deep shade and make for an intimate atmosphere in what is a large garden.

First, one comes to a small paved area with steps down from the back of the house. It is laid out formally, with four dwarf rose trees underplanted with mixed hardy geranium. Hardy fuchsia in pots complete the neat and tidy picture, but *Campanula garganica* has escaped into the grey stone wall placing itself naturally and perfectly. There are many shrub roses close by including *Rosa moyesii* and *R.rubrifolia*, both excellent in the stoney, poor soil.

The old vegetable garden has better conditions, having been improved over many years, and here the owners of Pen-y-Wern decided to plant a formal rose garden when they realized that half the produce remained uneaten. All sixty roses are of the old-fashioned shrub variety, climbers, or the 'new', Old English roses bred by David Austin, with all the qualities of the shrub roses. Roses can be somewhat amorphous as a group unless placed carefully. At Pen-y-Wern a circle of heavy rope swags supports the climbers, while a lavender hedge has been planted underneath to define the garden. The central point, where two gravel paths bisect, is the site for an iron gazebo covered with four well-grown clematis, including Lasurstern, distinguished by having the largest flowers of any hybrid.

Quite my favourite area is a pond garden at the lowest point in the grounds. The aforementioned beech hedge and surrounding shrubs give it a secret, enclosed air, and the whole tiny garden is dominated by an overhanging *Rosa* Nevada. This beautiful white shrub rose needs room to expand, but if you do have a space about eight feet by eight feet, it would be my first choice, even if there is only one fabulous flowering.

The old Victorian garden runs along the south eastern and western sides of the house. One reaches it by a flight of steps and pretty iron gate, to be met by the largest and finest copper beech I have ever seen. Two hundred and fifty feet in

The new rose garden at Pen-y-Wern.

69

circumference, at least 150 years old, it is both a delight and a problem, as it shades and dries out a huge area close to the house. Wisely, the owners have adapted to its ways and made a long *Iris sibirica* bed in the sunniest part of the garden, the area under the influence of the great tree having a shaded, oval bed filled with vigorous rampant foliage plants which can stand, or even appreciate, the difficult conditions.

There is so much in this garden of gardens, island beds in sun and shade on the big lawn; more beautiful and unusual trees, especially a large weeping beech of weird and mysterious shape. A white garden and a small terraced area full of fine grit for tiny alpine treasures. As we left, I noted the old-fashioned brilliant red *Pelargonium* Paul Crampel in simple terracotta pots placed on steps up to a weathered barn, while self-sown daisy flowers filled the cracks between. A lovely combination of artifice and nature, which somehow summed up for me everything which gardening, and this garden in particular, is all about.

Powis Castle Garden - Powys

Possibly one of the most important and impressive historic terraced gardens in Britain. Now owned by the National Trust and open regularly throughout the year, also under the National Garden Scheme (see Yellow Book).

The Italianate terraced gardens at Powis, built in rose-pink brick almost the same shade as the stone castle above them, are a fortunate survival. Since they were blasted from the ridge in the last years of the seventeenh-century, they have endured neglect, many changes of ownership, and even a plan to blow them up with gunpowder and replace them with a simple slope of turf in keeping with the fashion of the time. Fortunately, such 'improving' was confined to the park.

Early pictures show the now huge yews which dominate the terraces, small and neatly clipped. They are still meticulously attended to, but have grown into bulging, organic shapes with overhanging ridges like the eaves of a thatched cottage. For me, much of the charm of Powis is in the contrast between the dense green of the yews, and the warm pink of the brick walls.

The south-west slope against which the terraces nestle is sunny and sheltered from cold winds, but also very dry. There is a backbone of permanent planting both shrubby and herbaceous, but in recent years, this has been supplemented by tender perennials which are hardy only in the mildest winters. Osteospermum for example, is a notable feature in the top terrace. I have had the common white form and the dark pink in sheltered, well-drained spots in my own cold garden for many years, but such treasures as Buttermilk, a creamy-yellow; Whirligig, with spoon-shaped petals;and Blue Streak, white with a blue reverse, would probably have to be renewed four years out of five in any Border garden.

Artemisia 'Powis Castle', with subtle, greeny-grey foliage, overhangs the highest walls close to the castle. It was discovered at Powis, named in 1972, and is reasonably hardy there.

The second terrace, named the Aviary, after the open fronted building to the rear, is as memorable for perfume as colour. It was here, I first smelt the deliciously scented *Rhododendron*

The dramatic site of Powis Castle is clearly shown from the old orchard garden.

'Lady Alice Fitzwilliam', which is planted in a soil filled trough to take advantage of the cool, dampness inside. The gloomy, dank walls seem to intensify the scent, especially when it is hot and dry outside. Once experinced it is never forgotten, the perfume from my own plant inevitably conjuring up a memory of Powis. Outside are the shepherds and shepherdesses which decorate the balustrade and are contemporary with the terraces – the former now sadly depleted in number.

One descends to the Orangery Terrace which is broader, giving scope for wider borders which are at their best later in the year. Half hardy perennials here, include penstemons, alstroemerias, and dahlias. My particular favourite *Dahlia* 'Bishop of Llandaff', with scarlet flowers set off by dark bronze foliage, looks outstanding. The tender yellow *Rosa banksiae* 'Lutea', is also a feature, as are *Abutilon vitifolium* in mauve and white. The latter make only medium sized shrubs usually, but against the protecting walls at Powis, they are much taller.

A lovely colour grouping on the lower terrace includes an unusual, mauve shaded, *Lupinus aboreus*; *Erysimum* 'Bowles Form', the perennial purple wallflower; white *Anthemis punctata cupaniana* and *Olearia phlogopappa* 'Comber's Blue'. The latter is very tender, only to be attempted in the most favourable sites, and looks like a large, blue, Michaelmas daisy.

With a southerly aspect and sheltered site, it is not surprising that ceanothus do particularly well at Powis, thriving against the terrace walls. Again, their intense blue contrasts exceptionally well with the background pinky-grey. It is worth noting, that in less favoured places, the deciduous form, *C.X delileanus* 'Gloire de Versailles', with pale blue, feathery flowers, late in the year, is generally thought to be hardier than the evergreen kinds,

Bulging, organic yew hedges mark the end of the top terrace at Powis Castle Garden.

As the twentieth century dawned, the garden at Powis had been gradually deteriorating for many years, It was Violet, wife of the 4th Earl, who had both the ambition and taste to begin a great renewal. She was responsible for the formal gardens to the north-east of the large, lower lawn. This open, spacious garden, is best viewed from the terraces, and is reached by way of a path edged with great, undulating hedges of box, twenty feet high, as carefully trimmed as the yews.

A gently sloping lawn with pyramidal fruit trees each in its own round bed, greets ones eye as you emerge from the shelter of the box walk. The underplanting is imaginative and varied in both colour and texture. Soft, furry, *Stachys byzantina*, better known as Lamb's Lugs; the spiky, blue grass, *Festuca glauca*; golden marjoram: the viola, Irish Molly, with its unique, yellow-green and black colouring: as well as the double blue muscari, and *Ornithogalum nutans*, a subtle green and white, two beautiful but little known bulbs. Best of all, *Ophiopogon planiscapus* 'Nigrescens', black grass studded with pink tulips. The whole orchard slope is backed by an informal bank of shrubs and small trees, with wild flowers in the long grass. This is an excellent way to treat such an area, as daffodils also flourish there in the spring, and the grass cannot be cut until the leaves die back. There are many superb forest trees at Powis, as well as yet another formal garden, consisting of two lawns bisected by a path leading to an intricate, iron gate. Battlemented hedges surround, and there is a minimal arrangement within of upturned pudding basin yews. A central fountain is the only ornament. Perfectly simple, or just perfect, as is the whole garden at Powis.

Radnor Cottage - Shropshire

A two acre hilly garden, recently developed for all-year-round interest. Open under the National Gardens Scheme (see Yellow Book).

Radnor Cottage is a young garden made slowly and surely, though the owners have now retired and are able to spend more time at their favourite occupation. The cottage sits half way down a steep sided valley, with wonderful views over to the other side. Like knights of old in their castles, the owners can see all visitors approaching from far away. Wisely, they have conceived a layout which not only takes account of the slope, but includes several sitting out places to admire the hills.

The area closest to the house has an interesting flat bed, planted out with a delightful collection of low growing perennials enjoying the well drained soil. All were chosen to look good even in the winter, many with evergreen or grey foliage, and showing contrasts in leaf shape and colour when out of bloom. The mainstay of this border are the Rock roses, helianthemums, all grown from a packet of seed, and looking quite as colourful as many expensive, named varieties. Two plants impressed me in particular, a well grown, mature, *Ceanothus thyrsiflorus repens*, the prostrate ceanothus, covered with pale blue flowers and again grown inexpensively from a cutting. Also a superb, butter-yellow cheiranthus, the perennial wallflower, unfortunately name unknown. Other plants chosen not to obstruct the views include thymes; pinks; dwarf hardy geranium such as Ballerina, with a veined pink flower; low alpine phlox, and a hedge of *lavandula* 'Hidcote', quite the neatest for a small plot. On the paved terrace itself, sempervivums in pots make a lovely show.

Another terrace, with a seat built into a retaining, backing wall against the hill, was constructed by the male half of the partnership with rocks found on the site (of which there were plenty) and the debris from an old demolished house. This is a most successful conception, warm all the season through, as it faces due south and has shelter from the hill. Planting not only fills and spills out of the spaces left in the terrace, but also extends into the dry stone wall at the back. Because there is a backing of earth, plants do very well indeed, in fact sometimes rather too well and have to be chopped hard back. I liked the choice very much, especially the mixing of aesthetically good to look at (and smell) herbs, with sun lovers such as phormium – the New Zealand Flax, santolina and senecio, potentillas, more cistus, and the half-hardy osteospermum. Fifty plus varieties of plant have been found accommodation in the wall itself, especially sedums and encrusted saxifraga, which must have good drainage.

Not all the garden hugs the ground, in fact I thought one of the most imaginative plantings was in the large sloping field to the front of the house, which started as an orchard with many interesting fruit trees, even a medlar – then metamorphosed into a mini arboretum as the owners continued down the hill. I was delighted to see many native trees – sorbus, oaks and yew as well

The ideal use for surplus stone from an old building.

as chestnut, acers, even a strange yellow ash; though the marshier area on the other side of the drive does have more exotic trees such as *Taxodium distichum*, Swamp cypress, and a Ginkgo. The latter, in my opinion, hard to beat for autumn colour.

There is a pond, with a good selection of water loving plants, as well as other borders, but the overall impression left with me, was of a house and garden fitting so well into the landscape, that it was difficult to tell where one ended and the other began.

River House - Wrexham

A small, intimate garden, with an unrivalled collection of small trees, shrubs and herbaceous perennials. Open under the National Gardens Scheme (see Yellow Book).

The season at River House starts early with the crocus, gathers momentum with the cherry blossom and daffodils, then continues unabated throughout the whole year, ending just a few weeks before the crocus begin again with a display of winter flowering shrubs. Try as one might, it is impossible to visit this garden without finding not just one treasure, but a whole well considered planting in flower or, in the event of iron hard frost, in promising bud.

The garden is not large, about one acre, and slopes gently in the direction of the River Dee. It is fairly conventional in design. A circular drive at the front around the afore mentioned crocus and daffodils shaded by the cherries and a well-tended, wide lawn to the rear merging into flower beds mixed with mature shrubs and small trees, But any gardener worthy of the name, after just one glance at the superb suffruticosa tree peony close to the house, with immense, double lilac flowers, or the extraordinary *Paeonia delavayi* near an iron gate, with double, ruby-wine red flowers and blue-grey foliage, would know immediately that this is no ordinary garden.

The plants have been collected for nearly fifty years with an assured eye for the beautiful and a keen regard for the unusual. Many were obtained as cuttings or seeds from friends, and therefore revive personal memories as well as being pleasurable in their own right. The wonderful variegated elm in the garden, *Ulmus procera,* cv. Argenteo-variegata, is a case in point. The parent was a tree eighty feet high, which sadly died of Dutch Elm disease. The stump produced several suckers, which were pronounced infected and not likely to thrive. The owner of River House succeeded with every one she removed, and now has a specimen over twenty feet high of this exceedingly rare tree. A fine elaeagnus – believed to be *E. commutata* – flourishes in the small arboretum on the periphery of the garden. It has silver foliage on slender branches, miniature golden flowers, and scents the whole area when in bloom I have never seen another specimen, even in a botanic garden.

The lilies are superb, and the owner assures me, picked up for a song. It was at River House that I first made the acquaintance of the pimpinelli folia roses, delightful, miniature pompoms on full sized bushes in red, mauve, yellow, pink and white.

This garden is very much more than a collection of plants however. Colours, and combinations of flowers and foliage shape are well thought out, though self-seeding is both allowed and even encouraged. Spectacular groups include a yellow foliage theme of *Philadelphus coronarius* 'Aureus'; a fascinating form of *Rubus cockburnianus* with yellow leaves; white foxgloves and a small acer with yellow leaves backed by giant stands of angelica, that most statuesque of herbs, the whole stitched together by self-sown Bowles' golden grass. Nearby in the purple border, I noted *Anthriscus sylvestris* 'Raven's Wing', a black-leaved form of Queen Anne's Lace with pinky-white flowers; a new dark euphorbia, again never seen by me before; *Acer palmatum*, in an outstanding purple form; deep red berberis; and *Corylus maxima* 'Purpurea', the purple leaf hazel. The 'stitching' plant here is *Viola labradorica*, a self-seeding mauve violet with dark leaves. The essential different highlight comes from *Heuchera* 'Pewter Plate', playing the same contrast role as the white foxgloves in the yellow border.

The herb angelica, a statuesque plant for the back of the border.

I could go on, but readers will have guessed by now that this is one of the very few gardens that I would willingly swop for my own.

Strawberry Cottage - Herefordshire

A recently created, two acre cottage garden with many diverse areas and a wide variety of plants. Open under the Natinal Gardens Scheme (see Yellow Book).

This is a new garden surrounding an old house that was once a smallholding. The owners only moved in six years ago, and were immediately faced with a number of problems which they proceeded to turn into assets.

The first difficulty was the sloping site, exacerbated by a quarry-like cliff very close to the house which the previous owner had excavated as a car park! Weeds and debris choked the bank, and it is perpetually wet from two small springs which surface half way down. As it is in full view from the cottage windows, this was one of the first parts worked on, and the chief object was to provide colour and foliage interest over a long period. Daffodils begin the season, but when we visited in early July, hostas, geums, spiraea, mimulus, primula and hemerocallis were all in full flower. The two springs make the area wet even in the summer, so damp lovers do well,

Trellis and posts give height in a new garden, as well as providing places for climbing plants.

but osteospermum and dianthus also looked vigorous and happy. After their work of supplying moisture to the bank, the springs are diverted around the cottage to a small pond, and then allowed to trickle out to make a bog garden.

Fierce winds blow from the east in winter time, so another priority was a shelter belt of laurel close to the cottage. The large shiny leaves are very attractive, but must be cut individually with pruners, otherwise, if mangled and chopped by shears, lose half their beauty.

The garden is filled with interesting and imaginative touches; stonecrop in the drive, softening the hard surface. An old mill stone half hidden by an ivy, the small, dark green, yellow centred Gold Heart. An oblong, paved courtyard, well away from the house, with a bird bath and a pergola hung with the pink edged rose Handel. In fact, if I had to pick just one plant to write about at Strawberry Cottage, it would be the roses. The owners are passionately fond of all kinds, and I think that I can safely say that every type is represented among over two hundred grown. There are shrub, miniature and patio roses also climbers and ramblers on the many trellis boundries and pergolas. The owners use these to give height in a garden which, because of its youth, lacks mature trees at this stage. H. T. roses are not left out, but, because they are used in combination with other shrubs and types of roses, avoid that stiff, municipal look, serried ranks of hard pruned H. T. roses grown on their own seem to adopt.

A favourite spot for me, is a depression which was once an archaeological site where an old wall was excavated. It has been left almost untouched, though the wall can now hardly be seen for the plants, and adapted to make a rock garden with a sitting-out place. The Romans inhabited all this area of the Borderlands, and a Roman bath was found in an adjoining field. This kind of local history must certainly lend spice to the winter digging!

The large lawn close by has several island beds carved out to make open, sunny places to grow more shrub roses. They are subject to cold winds, but are carefully chosen to combat the elements. Cerise Bouquet has been a great success, as has *Rosa rubrifolia*, with very purple foliage in full sun. This part of the garden cannot be that cold, because I was astonished to find a tall eucalyptus was only three years old.

More trellis separates further beds up the slope cut in an interesting radiating pattern, each segment given over to a different colour. This field was only purchased a few years ago and is very young as yet, but the owners have avoided putting shrubs and perennials too close for instant effect, using annuals such as pansies to fill out until the permanent planting gets underway.

There is an excellent vegetable garden at the cottage, also a wild part with newly planted sorbus, buddleia, and malus to encourage birds and butterflies, The pond is already filled with frogs and fish, an ingenious trip wire round the edge forcing the local herons to look but not touch. In fact, this garden lacks nothing that time, effort, and a real love of plants can bring to it.

Three Chimneys - Wrexham

A forester's garden of one acre, packed with an extraordinary collection of small trees. Open under the National Gardens Scheme (see Yellow Book).

Three Chimneys is one of the most unusual and distinctive gardens I have ever seen, as the owners live in the middle of a miniature forest. Although only yards from the road, the original bungalow can hardly be observed beneath the canopy of trees both coniferous and deciduous. The owner was once a forester, and resolved, when he moved in thirty-seven years ago, to recreate his ideal landscape from the one acre of cow pasture around his house.

Autumn at Three Chimneys provides as much colour as springtime in other gardens.

The autumn colours from the many acers in the garden are quite superb. They are planted almost like perennials in large groups, very close together, so that one colour blends with another in the manner of a large herbaceous bed. Very few of the huge collection of trees are named varieties, the owner preferring to grow them – the Japanese acers especially – from seed. He also has the expertise to graft and take cuttings. This does not seem to matter however, many of the forms at Three Chimneys are quite as striking as expensive, named varieties. A few I did recognize were: *Cornus nuttallii* 'Gold Ring', and *C.florida* 'Rainbow', both with good variegation. Also the variegated symphoricarpos, the Snowberry, not very interesting in the plain green form, but absolutely delightful when each oval leaf is edged with gold. Among the many very unusual trees raised in the garden, is a variegated Coffee tree, *Gymnocladus dioicus* 'Variegata', its beautiful large leaves having a creamy-white edge,

The colourful deciduous trees are set off by an equally good collection of conifers, again, many rare, and/or difficult to both grow well, and propagate. I made the acquaintance of *Pinus strobus* 'Nana', a tiny pine which develops into a dense bush, and learnt that no two plants raised from seed are ever quite the same. The foliage variety in the conifers at Three Chimneys is extraordinary, from yellow threads, to needle pines and flat, glossy holly leaves, again in every shade of green from the yellow to the blue range, The owner is a mine of information on every tree in his garden, the sort that can only be acquired after a lifetimes experience. The name Snake-bark maple for example, covers a whole group of trees with beautifully striped bark, but can only easily be raised from seed in the form *Acer pensylvanicum*, though most people acknowledge that *A.hersii* is the best form.

Walking around the forest glades (although only an acre, I cannot think of the garden as anything other than a forest) flashes of colour-orange, red, brilliant butter-yellow and dusky pink, stand out from the general background at every turn in the gravel and log path. Sometimes berries add to the medley – skimmia, cotoneaster, and sorbus; once a large oblong pool, its surface patterned with maple leaves, suddenly came into view behind a thick thuja hedge.

The owner loves his trees, and keeps discovering others he wishes to grow, creating a more and more colourful, congested wonderland. He did try bulbs early in the gardens history, to vary the scene, but most were devoured by squirrels, or simply found the competition too much. I suspect the owner was quite pleased, as it left more room for his beloved trees.

If an other plant does get a chance, it is the climbers, which can of course, find their own way to light and air. I loved the great, twisted wisteria, and could only marvel at the notoriously difficult *Tropaeolum speciosum*, with brilliant scarlet flowers, which at Three Chimneys has to be pulled out in handfuls to prevent it overgrowing its neighbours.

Tir-y-Fron - Wrexham

A one and three quarter acre garden, which includes an old quarry, packed with rare and interesting plants, Open under the National Gardens Scheme (see Yellow Book).

With the great bank of Offa's Dyke running along one side of the drive, Tir-y-Fron is as Border a garden as one can possibly imagine. The garden appears large, and its position is close to the rolling hills around Llangollen without being domin-ated by them: the whole made secluded by a periphery of mature forest trees – limes, beech and yew. It is however, the plants which flourish within the ring of trees and in an old quarry which make this beautiful garden memorable.

Some gardens just grow, and this is how Tir-y-Fron came into being, the owners working outwards from the house over a period of fourteen years. They found two lawns, one above the other at the rear of the house, with a flight of steps and some terracing between, H. T. roses being the only plants of any significance. The terracing and steps remain, but a bank of low herbaceous perennials, chosen chiefly for their wonderful foliage, now fills the space once occupied by the roses. The plants are packed closely so that not a speck of earth shows between, and are not planted in groups, but repeated many times on both sides of the steps, giving a homogeneous whole and preventing the display looking one sided. Mainstays, are the hardy *Geranium renardii*, one of

A well planted border at Tir-y-Fron.

the best for foliage effect with pretty grey/green leaves, also *G.clarkei* 'Kashmir White'. *Alchemilla mollis* can be a little too much of a good thing in this kind of tightly packed border, but is too beautiful in flower and foliage to leave out. Astrantia is that other cottage garden favourite which seeds prolifically and can quickly take over a border if not kept under strict control. A lovely touch close to the steps on either side are plants of *Cotoneaster horizontalis* 'Variegatus', grown to soften the edges. When we visited most colour came from the almost hardy osteospermums, especially the form with a white flower which sprawls attractively, flowers all summer non stop, and is as tough as any hebe.

The soil in the garden is very variable, as it is close to an old industrial area. Large patches of heavy clay give way to fertile loam, while the old quarry is shaly. Past liming also gives a different P. H., with azaleas possible in some parts of the garden. It tends to be dry, with fierce winds from the direction of the Welsh mountains, but tempered by the high trees and a number of old walls and outbuildings.

The quarry is a deep hole some way from the house, which was completely derelict when the owners took over, and provided an opportunity to really experiment. They had no idea whether it would be damp or dry, and proceeded by trial and error to create a truly beautiful composition, separate from and very different in character from the rest of the garden. It turned out to be on the dry side, even at the bottom, and a huge beech with exposed roots overhanging the area did not help. Ligularia, rodgersia, rheum, and water loving grass were already in and doing reasonably well. If things get too dry in a hot summer, the owners flood the hollow to help things along. Most of the steep banks are terraced with slatey stones found on site, but the thousands of old bricks dug up crumbled in the first frosts, and proved useless.

There are many old favourites mixed with new cultivars in this part of the garden, but the early flat roses such as moyesii, red; Canary Bird, yellow; and cinnamomea, red with a paler centre, are all spectacular in the poor soil, while climbers such as Handel enjoy the better conditions nearer the house.

Much is made of trellis, painted an effective dull green, to divide one part of the garden from another, and every bit is hung with clematis, honeysuckle, roses, and almost every other hardy climber that one can think of. A clematis completely new to me, a delicate white single in a sheltered position is *Clematis forsteri*.

There is little formal planning, but the garden works wonderfully well as a whole, each area blending into another. Some colour arranging is attempted, and the owner is not afraid of moving plants around until she finds just the correct position. I am coming to the conclusion that gardening is an art, very like music or painting, that one is born with – gardens owned by these talented people standing out vividly from the rest.

ᗝorwood - Herefordshire

A small, interesting garden, containing conifers, shrubs, herbacious plants and water features. Open under the National Gardens Scheme (see Yellow Book).

Torwood is a small garden, whose owners (when they moved in fourteen years ago) were determined to forgo no gardening pleasure because of the size of their plot. The tiny front garden is filled with trees both deciduous and coniferous. Most are varieties that gardeners would consider right for small areas – *Acer dissectium* and *Robinia pseudocacia* 'Frisia' for example, but other such as *Cedrus deodara*, make no concessions to size. The owners are unruffled by thoughts of the future, enjoying the trees while young, and fully prepared to prune or remove when necessary. In fact, enjoyment is what this garden is all about. It gives creative interest to its owners, visitors revel in the flower filled rear garden, it is even involved in educational projects with the junior school next door. All the children filing over in the spring time to collect plants propagated by the owners of Torwood for planting out in the childrens own gardens at the school.

Although sited in a delightful part of the country close to Ross on Wye, the garden is in close proximity to a busy road. To help deaden the traffic noise, a baffling hedge of conifers lines the front garden on the road side. At the rear, there is less protection, but a gravel garden at the side of the house is an oasis of tranquility. Once again the owners have fitted much into a small space. A wooden summerhouse, a large and beautiful mature cherry tree, pots of all descriptions – some filled with colourful begonias, others (when we paid a late visit) crammed with hosta in autumn shades of yellow.

Every area of the garden seems to have a small water garden of its own, you even approach it over a river flowing in a deep culvert, but the pond in the rear garden is especially successful. It is a raised pool, its sides planted up with sedum, Lamb's lugs, *Campanula garganica*, and the smaller, running euphorbia. This particular pond is a haven for wild life, being full of newts, frogs, insects and fish.

The owners of Torwood spend little money on their garden, growing everything in it (and it was empty when they arrived) from seed or cuttings supplied by friends and neighbours. This is hard to believe when one notes the quality of the plants on view. There is a well grown *Arbutus x andrachnoides*, the Strawberry tree, only for a sheltered position away from the south and west, which will cover itself with strawberry-like red fruits in the autumn if it approves your garden. Also *Fremontia californicum*, a very vigorous shrub wth dark green leaves and bright yellow flowers which are produced from spring to autumn, but again only for a warm wall.

Michaelmas daisies en mass at Torwood.

There is a truly beautiful collection of Michaelmas daisies in the rear garden, ranging from white and the palest mauve, through dark mauve, purple, all the blues and true pinks. How much more effective they are grouped together in one bed, and in a variety of heights, rather than scattered all over the garden where they lose half their impact, Also at the back, is a small pergola covered in clematis, honeysuckle, and to save space, a loganberry. Winter and autumn interest had been considered in the shape of the climbing nasturtium, *Tropaeolum tuberosum* 'Ken Aslet', and the fluffy seed heads of *Clematis tangutica*.

The small conservatory is a microcosm of the whole garden, with a superb – and rare – Norfolk Island pine (a tender conifer), a bougainvillea still in flower in October, and a wonderful display of fuchsia in baskets.

Tyn-y-Graig - Denbighshire

A hillside garden of approximately one and a half acres, incorporating six, descending, landscaped pools. Open under the National Gardens Scheme (see Yellow Book).

Tyn-y-Graig can best be described as a water garden, because the whole of the lower slope before the house consists of a chain of six pools, fed by a natural stream, and dug from the stony clay in the past eight to ten years, The slope is steep, but a series of gentle waterfalls leads the stream from one pond to another. The last and lowest, boasts clever miniature lock gates to

A garden of water at Tyn-y-Graig, natural streams channelled from top to bottom.

control the flow of water, diverting it away from the pond to an overflow stream when there are floods.

The ponds are separated by narrow grass and gravel paths, as well as several flights of ankle-breaking, natural stone stairs. Every step one takes seems to be either up or down, there is very little level terrain in the whole garden.

Planting is simple and effective, mostly in large groups, so as not to distract from the beautiful countryside all around. *Alchemilla mollis, Lysimachia nummularia*, (Creeping Jenny) and saxifragas. There are 'country' trees – hawthorn, alder, hazel and sycamore, which, together with the dry stone walls, blend well with the surrounding hills. I particularly admired the very large stand of *Cotoneaster horizontalis* grown as ground cover on an almost vertical slope. Very effective, and perfect for the position. A hedge of *Berberis darwinii* separates the garden from the adjoining paddock. It was clipped severely when we visited which usually inhibits flowering, but at Tyn-y-Graig was in full bloom.

In spite of the draining effect of the ponds, the lower part of the garden is still extremely boggy. Here is a wonderful example of going 'with' your garden, and exploiting its natural assets instead of fighting them. A stand of alder giving light shade has been underplanted with our native primrose *Primula vulgaris*, Marsh Marigolds *Caltha palustris*; blue ajuga, astilbe and candelabra primroses. No attempt has been made to over garden the area and large moss covered rocks are left protruding from the ground add greatly to the beauty of the scene.

As befits such a damp garden, there is an impressive collection of hostas in a variety of leaf shape and colours. Hosta take many years to make really big clumps, but the conditions at Tyn-y-Graig are obviously ideal for maximum growth. Hosta are easy to grow given a little shade, a plentiful supply of moisture, and some success in controlling your slug population. They will in fact survive in fairly dry places, but never make the luxuriant growth seen at Tyn-y-Graig unless well watered.

One knows that the ponds are dug by hand in this garden, and the waterfalls man made, but because of the natural source of water and the use of stone cut from the hill the house and garden stands upon, the whole effect is natural and unaffected. The views are superb from every point, one range of hills giving way to another as you ascend the slope back to the house. The sheets of bluebells in the wood close by and along the rough bank near the house, echoing the misty colour of the distant mountains.

The Walled Garden - Powys

A three acre walled garden, with stream, bog garden, herbaceous perennials and shrubs. Open under the National Gardens Scheme (see Yellow Book).

The name walled garden, describes itself, but it could equally well be called the river garden. The Hindwell Brook (no brook in my opinion, but a fair sized river) forms one boundry of the garden, causing both pleasure and pain to gardeners on the site. Its moisture is very welcome to irrigate the quick draining loam in a dry year, not so welcome when it floods half the big lawn and threatens the house.

The garden originated as the walled kitchen plot of a large mansion, and it is the remaining high, warm brick walls and grey stone arches, which form the bones of this beautiful garden. Wisely, the owners have not fought the naturally boggy conditions but have specialized in plants which enjoy a moist rootrun, or even actually getting their feet wet.

A beautiful raised pool at the Walled Garden.

One approaches the garden past an ancient church and through deciduous woods, until a steep slope to the river, a fine *Acer pseudoplatanus*, 'Prinz Handjery', and a buttressed wall marks the beginning of the garden proper. Here an oblong lawn surrounds a rose bed with a wide border of weathered tiles. Two other superb small trees in this area include a well placed weeping copper beech, and a Judas tree, *Cercis siliquastrum*. The latter was covered in promising buds which expand in late spring to produce clusters of bright pink flowers, and, in a good summer, purple pods later in the year. The walls in this part of the garden required extensive work, but all have been repaired with old materials, which blend well with the existing structure.

With so many walls offering space for climbers facing every aspect, it is no surprise to find excellent specimens of wisteria, early *Clematis montana* in various forms, climbing roses to come, and that perfect wall plant, *Cytisus battandieri*. The latter has pineapple scented, lemon coloured flowers, set against grey/green leaves, and can only be grown successfully in a sheltered position, preferably against a warm wall. Not rare or choice, but looking absolutely right, is a plant of common ivy, its glossy leaves half hiding a wall-hung dovecote. These great walls around the main garden, must once have been the background for tender stone fruits such as apricot and peach, but tree peonies, *Chaenomeles japonica*, and camellia have now taken their place.

Behind one of the main walls, shaded by large shrubs, is a small ditch which has been dammed to make a bog garden extending right around to the front of the house. When we visited in late spring, that great standby of the wet garden, candelabra primroses, were making a colourful show, but I also liked the big clumps of *Polygonum bistorta* 'Superbum', covered in pale pink pokers, and proving what an excellent plant it can be when well grown with plenty of moisture. Another favourite noted, was *Ranunculus aconitifolius* 'Flore Pleno', the white double buttercup. It is hard to get hold of, as demand far exceeds supply, but is well worth the effort to track down, as no more delightful plant for a damp spot exists. The single form is also pretty, as is the double yellow meadow buttercup, but the latter does better in a well-drained situation.

The garden is necessarily one of strong shapes and definite plan, because of the architectural background, with lawns and terrace beautifully tended, though the edges of the bog garden have been allowed to take on a wilder note with self sown primula, ferns and filipendula. A bank overlooking the ditch has a mingled tapestry of *Brunnera macrophylla* in forget-me-not blue, our native red campion and white scabious, or Queen Anne's Lace, absolutely beautiful, and a lovely contrast to the more formal parts of the garden.

ᴓhe ᴕeir Gardens - ᴕerefordshire

A large and unique garden situated on a steep bank of the River Wye. Owned by the National Trust and open in season every Wednesday to Sunday inclusive. Tel: (01684) 850051.

The Weir Gardens are really the setting for a riverside walk along the Wye, and stretch from a sharply angled dog-leg bend with huge concrete river defences, to the car park at the other end of the garden. The eighteenth-century house (which is not open to the public) is at the top of the slope.

The gardens are laid out on a very steep incline, with many paths both up and down and alongside the water. A flight of steps so narrow you have to progress sideways, brings you right on to the river bank, with Old Man's Beard, our native clematis, dipping its fingers into the water, while iridescent blue dragon-flies swoop and hover over the slow moving river. When the Wye is calm and low, green strands of weed like long hair moves slowly with the current, but heavy rain can turn it into a torrent which reaches to the top of the concrete banks.

So steep is the slope from house to river, many of the paths up and down have decorative handrails, while underfoot, wooden planks held by pegs make rough steps in keeping with the natural feel of the gardens. At one point, a wooden walkway in the sky, like a one sided bridge, carries you over a particularly precipitous slope. Below, a waterfall of St. Johns Wort, hypericum, flows downwards to the river bank. The view is breathtaking, across the Wye to tranquil countryside, with the Black Mountains making an impressive backdrop.

The rock garden is the most intensively cultivated part of the Weir Garden.

The gardens were originally laid out in the 1920s, when they would have been a good deal more formal than they are today. There is still a charming rockery from this period, none the less beautiful for being at one with the wilder aspects of the garden, and supporting pinks, hardy geranium and ferns, as well as mature, well shaped, Japanese maples. The tall, dark, pointed junipers are a perfect contrast to the airy, gold foliage of the acers. There are many magnificent trees in the garden, through the branches of which the flat, glittering river is constantly sighted as you make your way up and down. This is gardening on a grand scale with tree shapes and colours. Poplar, spruce, larch, chestnuts, oak, birch and ash all grow in the garden, as well as more exotic shrubs closer to the house. The glory of the garden however, is its display of early bulbs, grown naturally in woodland glades and among the hardy ground cover. In the spring, daffodils of all descriptions vie with the smaller

bulbs such as the blue chionodoxa, *Scilla siberica*, and *Ipheion uniflorum*. Later, narcissi, bluebells and tulips take over. The tall blue *Camassia leichtlinii* seeds everywhere to make a wonderful display in mid to late April. This largely unknown bulb comes from America, and, if it likes your gardens conditions (good soil and not too dry) will soon be coming up in every nook and cranny.

With such a wealth of trees and shrubs, as well as an abundance of water, the gardens are a perfect wild life habitat with birds and insects often sighted, while wild flowers abound. The area is managed with conservation very much in mind, the grass carefully cut when flowers have seeded – not before. There are few formal buildings in the garden, but mention must be made of an extraordinary little summerhouse, the floor laid with horses' teeth in a mosaic-like pattern. Also a depression in the ground shored up with Roman bricks, which was once thought to be a Holy Well.

This is a truly unique garden, with a wonderfully secluded atmosphere. I shall long remember the wild flowers – valerian, tansy, great clumps of sun-bleached

The River Wye runs the whole length of the garden.

grass and willows overhanging the river, where the only disturbance was the circles made by rising fish.

Welsh College of Horticulture - Flintshire

Large mature gardens, incorporating a variety of different areas, planned to give the students experience at every branch of horticulture. Open under the National Gardens Scheme (see Yellow Book).

The Welsh College of Horticulture exists to provide courses in all branches of horticulture, from environmental and conservation work to floristry, and touching almost every aspect of gardening in between.

The grounds cover a large area, over three hundred and fifteen acres, including the main college building built in utilitarian style of brick, but softened by Virginia creeper and imaginative planting close against the walls. There are glass houses by the hectare, a garden machinery department, floristry and dried flower area, organic garden; even the colleges own plant centre where the general public can buy the results the many students produce.

The beautifully planted grounds of the college are a valuable teaching aid, covering all aspects of gardening as well as being of considerable historical interest. The latter comes from two ancient monuments of Llys Edwin and Watt's Dyke, while woodland dates back to 1717 and contains fish ponds considerably older. The location of Watt's Dyke is of particular interest to me, as it runs close to the edges of my own garden, and together with Offa's Dyke, gives continuity to the whole Border land.

The grounds consist mainly of wide sweeping lawns, with some magnificent mature trees. There are individual cedars, both of deodara type and libani; a superb *Betula papyrifera*, and many large Japanese maples, It was the groups which impressed me however, groves of silver birch, alder and Scots pine, under planted with heathers and the small leaved rhododendron. I can only describe them as island beds of trees. The ground is broken up by huge shelter belts of Leyland cypress, and many areas have well grown shrub borders of rhododendron and groups of conifers in gold, blue and green. There is a strong emphasis on our native trees, but a touch of the oriental comes from a huge clump of bamboo. More shrubs include a dogwood, *cornus kousa* var.chinensis, covered, when we visited in June, with white flowers (or more strictly speaking bracts) grown as part of a double

Part of the Pool Garden at the Welsh College of Horticulture.

avenue backed by tall beech hedges with a focal point of a small wooden summerhouse at one end.

I think my favourite spot in the whole garden, is a big pond filled with floriferous water lilies in pink and white, as well as one of the very best clumps of the Arum lily, *Zantedeschia aethiopica* I have ever seen. This beautiful semi-hardy plant will often survive quite hard winters if it can get its feet right down into the water, where its roots are protected by the unfrozen mud. The group at the college must have contained over a hundred pure white, elegant trumpets, reflected in the water and set off by yellow Flag iris. Other damp loving plants clustered in and around the pond, include the striped grass *Miscanthus sinensis* 'Zebrinus', yellow loosestrife, *Alchemilla mollis, Iris sibirica*, hosta and dwarf willows. Seats to view the water garden back up against a raised bed, and are overhung with single pink roses grown to drape over the edges.

Close to the entrance and the main building is the bowling green, with a fine herbaceous border running along one side. Once again however, it was the shrub border which separates the grass from the front of the building which impressed. Massed silver and grey plantings from smaller shrubs such as senecio and ballota, contrasted with white potentillas, escallonias and cistus, all backed by taller, dark-green cotoneaster, and the red leaved *Berberis thunbergii*. Low plantings are mostly large spreads of osteospermum, in the hardiest silver/blue colour. Needless to say, with so many willing helpers and a dedicated ground staff, maintenance of the borders, indeed all of the grounds, is nothing less than perfect. I wish that I had so many free weeders.

Woodside Cottages - Shropshire

A small cottage garden full of interesting plants, with an especially fine collection of hardy geranium. Open under the National Gardens Scheme (see Yellow Book).

If I read out a list of the plants growing at Woodside Cottages, you might imagine a garden three times the size – there are one hundred and thirty two forms of hardy geranium alone. The owner however, has squeezed in more and more precious plants as her interest and expertise has grown. The result is a crowded garden no doubt, but the whole conception works wonderfully, every plant having room to breath, either leaning on, or shaded by a neighbour according to its individual preference.

Small size is the first problem in this garden, the second is shape. Woodside is long and narrow, with close neighbours on either side. Privacy is obtained by high fencing which also gives scope for many plants to be trained in an upward direction. The length of the garden is effectively disguised by a pergola hung with climbers; mainly ivies for complete, year round concealment, wisteria and clematis for beauty, and honeysuckle for scent.

The garden is bursting at the seams, not only with plants, but with good ideas. In the tiny front garden for example, an eclectic collection of holed containers are full of hosta, dwarf hardy geraniums and many more smaller plants which might get lost in the main garden. The pots are as interesting as the flowers – old buckets, watering cans, tin baths, and even a dolly-tub!

In the garden proper, the geraniums tie all the crowded planting to-gether. Out of the vast

A tapestry of low growing perennials at Woodside Cottages.

number grown, I must mention *Geranium sylvaticum* Amy Doncaster', a knee high, fairly new geranium which is the most beautiful, pure, sky-blue, with a white eye. It flowers over a long period and is quite one of the best recent introductions. *G.clarkei* 'Kashmir white', is an old favourite with white flowers veined in dark pink on a low, spreading plant. I would also recommend its sister, *G. c.* 'Kashmir Purple'. At Woodside, I saw Kashmir Pink, very new and just as good as the other two. All the hardy geraniums are trouble free plants, even the tall, straggling kinds like *G. phaeum*, can lean on taller com-panions, or be allowed to sprawl attractively. I have never known any of the group to be attacked by pests, they are very drought tolerant, and many will grow in fairly deep shade. For the latter position, I would suggest the aforementioned phaeum.

It has small flowers in rather dark shades of mauve or red, but there is a delightful white form, and needless to say, I saw at Woodside the very latest *G.phaeum* 'Samobar', with a variegation on the leaf. Just one more, *G. wallichianum* 'Buxton's Blue', a trailer this time, with white centred, pale-blue flowers, at its best on a raised bed where it can fall gracefully over the side, blooming in late August and September.

Not everything at Woodside happens at ground level, pittosporums with their delightfully crinkled foliage so good for flower arranging, bamboo, and a very large phormium with huge spiky leaves give a change of height and scale. There is also a fine example of the golden elm, *Ulmus x hollandica* 'Wredei', perfect for a small garden, being compact, slow growing, and a clear gold all summer.

The garden at Woodside ends in an awkward point, and the treatment given to this difficult area sums up the whole garden for me. Instead of hiding it, a prominent feature in the shape of a large, knarled tree trunk lies across the widest part, just allowing a glimpse around the corner. Holes in the wood are filled with earth, and support even more plants. This trunk was spotted from the top of a bus, the farmer rung up, and the log transported to its final resting place in double quick time. Nothing is too much trouble for the owner of Woodside, and it certainly shows.